PEAK

EXPERIENCES

BY

MANSON BOZE

Foreword by Tom Cecil

A MAN AND HIS SON FIND UNEXPECTED CHALLENGE,
ADVENTURE AND REWARD, ALONG WITH AN
AMAZING VENUE FOR BONDING, IN AN
ENVIRONMENT MANY NEVER EXPERIENCE.

First Printing

Copyright © 2013

All rights reserved. No part of this book may be reproduced or transmitted in any form or by any means, electronically or mechanical, including photocopying, recording, or by any information storage and retrieval system, without the written permission of the Publisher.

Author - Manson Boze

Publisher
Wayne Dementi
Dementi Milestone Publishing, Inc.
Manakin-Sabot, VA 23103
www.dementimilestonepublishing.com

Cataloging-in-publication data for this book is available from The Library of Congress.

ISBN: 978-0-9889099-5-3

Graphic design by:
Dianne Dementi

Printed in U.S.A.

Attempts have been made to identify the owners of any copyrighted materials appearing in this book. The publisher extends his apology for any errors or omissions and encourages copyright owners inadvertently missed to contact him.

Preface

The story of how a 56 year old man from Richmond, VA ended up at high camp on one of the biggest mountains in the world.

At 43, the author discovered a whole new avenue for adventure, exercise and bonding with his 6-year-old son. Fourteen years later, both are experienced climbers with dozens of exciting stories, shared experiences and a lifelong connection, with or without the rope they shared over the years.

Sheer rock walls hundreds of feet tall, big mountains, icy glaciers, storms, competitive rock climbing – experience all of this and more through the eyes of an everyday guy and his son as they explore the world of climbing.

The author learns that failure (to reach a summit) in the mountains can be just as rewarding as success – or more accurately that success means getting home safely after an exciting and enjoyable experience punctuated by good decisions along the way, regardless of whether the party reached the summit.

About Tom Cecil

*T*om was a lucky 13 year old when he was brought to Seneca Rocks on a climbing adventure with a family friend. Those two weeks in June 1973 changed his life forever.

Tom is about to spend his 40th year climbing and 26th year guiding at Seneca Rocks.

The following are a few of the milestones Tom is especially proud of:

- PCGI Lead Guide Certified
- Chosen by Garrett College in Western Maryland for over 15 years to develop and operate their Adventure-Sports Institute climbing instruction and guides' training program.
- Twenty-five+ (don't jinx me) years of accident-free multi-pitch guiding at Seneca.
- Completion of the TradWall & Anchoring Center at our guide service facilities at Seneca.
- Being asked by John Long to edit his latest anchoring treatise.
- Guiding in Europe, Mexico, Australia; more than 23 years spent pioneering new routes here at Seneca and in southern Thailand.

These days if you don't find Tom guiding a Seneca classic, teaching a Lead Course or training the guides you'll usually find him somewhere in the North Fork valley hanging out with the Mollster putting up first ascents and hoping to find another Triple S; while he may not find it today, it doesn't mean its not out there!

Foreword

*F*rom the first chapter of Manson's book I felt the camaraderie, the kinship of the rope, the shared journey that has come to symbolize the unspoken bond that unites virtually all climbers. This book is about that rare place we all hope to find - a place we feel a connection we can't describe. Among climbers it's known as "getting the bug" but it's a passion way beyond any bug. It's a clarity that comes from the hyper-focus that only real risk can bring – and which requires a high level of self-discipline. Without discipline the focus turns to paralysis – or panic – both of which are detrimental to success and often to safety. Manson and Austin are among the lucky few who found that connection one fateful day in the local climbing gym. For generations climbers have experienced this "kinship of the rope," a bond felt – not seen, a connection that forms the foundation for a life of adventure. It is a bond that makes it easy for climbers who have never met before to quickly form lasting friendships with one another. In short, climbing puts the rest of life in a different perspective.

What I find most gratifying is that, even with completely different introductions to climbing - Manson's and Austin's in an indoor climbing gym and mine outside - we still became members of the same tribe, a tribe that intuitively understands why you're willing to crawl out of a warm tent at 4:00 in the morning to climb a cold dark and possibly dangerous mountain. I expect this genre of book to grow as the popularity of indoor climbing creates more opportunity for people to try climbing.

I'm fortunate to call myself a professional climber. I actually make a living doing the thing I love. But you don't have to be a pro to love the sport, a theme that is evident throughout Manson's book. There is pure joy and satisfaction, along with many other emotions, in rock climbing and mountaineering. Some climb to impress, some to chase numbers (difficult ratings), but the real satisfaction is in the movement – and just being "out there" (or "in there" in the case of the gym). Austin seems to "get it" too, even though most of his climbing career thus far has been devoted to competitive climbing.

My view of climbing gyms has evolved over the 25 years since the first gyms opened in the United States. They offer a great introduction to climbing movement and a terrific venue for fun and exercise as well as skill, strength and technique development but I believe many miss out on what climbing could be when their only experience is indoors. Climbing outdoors adds much more dimension and adventure to the experience and has the potential for leading to a lifetime of ever-growing and changing exploration, much like it did for Manson. I'm encouraged to see that the siren song of the cliffs and mountains is still strong.

Climbing is constantly changing but the passion and drive which Manson and Austin are experiencing are the eternal characteristics of climbing's brotherhood – and that magical "connection." I hope you enjoy this book as much as I did and, if you haven't already, that you give our sport a go.

Tom Cecil
PCGI Certified Guide

TABLE OF CONTENTS

Preface iii
About Tom Cecil iv
Foreword v
Acknowledgements viii
Affirmations x
About the author xii
Prologue xv
Chapter 1 ~ In the Beginning 1
Chapter 2 ~ Our First Big Climbing Trip 7
Chapter 3 ~ Into the Rockies 17
Chapter 4 ~ The Adventure Continues 25
Chapter 5 ~ Austin is Invited to the National Championship 28
Chapter 6 ~ Adventures Close to Home 33
Chapter 7 ~ Competitive Climbing Starts to
              Come Into Its Own 35
Chapter 8 ~ Back to the Rockies 37
Chapter 9 ~ A National Champion! 47
Chapter 10 ~ Another Trip to the Rockies 51
Chapter 11 ~ Growing Ambitions for Father and Son 71
Chapter 12 ~ A Foray Into the Big League 81
Chapter 13 ~ Another National Championship 101
Chapter 14 ~ Growth and Challenge 105
Chapter 15 ~ New England Adventure 111
Chapter 16 ~ Busy Year 113
Chapter 17 ~ Back to Wyoming 119
Chapter 18 ~ An Uneventful Year 133
Chapter 19 ~ Growth on Several Fronts 137
Chapter 20 ~ Yosemite 141
Chapter 21 ~ Life Goes On 144
Chapter 22 ~ Steps Along the Way 149
Chapter 23 ~ Another Trip to Colorado 154
Chapter 24 ~ Growing Up and Moving On 167
Chapter 25 ~ Highs and Lows in the Rockies 179
Chapter 26 ~ Rocky Starts and a Big Next Step 199
Chapter 27 ~ Aconcague 215
Chapter 28 ~ Since Then 242

Acknowledgements

*T*here are many people who have been meaningful to me in various ways as I have explored the world of climbing. In fact almost everyone I have met through climbing has been both unique and special in some good way. First I'd like to thank the owners and staff of Peak Experiences Indoor Climbing Gym, Scott Powell, Kevin Tobin and Jay Smith in particular. The first day I walked in to their facility (to drop my son off for a birthday party) they welcomed me in to their community and invited me to give the sport a try. Kevin gave me my first instruction on climbing technique. I have spent many hours at Peak and even served as an instructor on their staff. Their gym is now in its 15th year and continues to be a beacon of teamwork, excellent customer service and unwavering attention to safety.

Others who have been instrumental in teaching me the ropes, sharing a campfire and/or sharing a rope (with all that means both literally and symbolically) include: Bill Trainor, Billy Salter, Adam Leftwich, Kirsten Kremer, Susanne Smith and Coop Cooperstein.

Thanks to Georgia Riddick, my former co-worker at the Chamber and a former English teacher who proofread my manuscript and provided valuable feedback.

A very big thank you to Tom Cecil, owner of Seneca Rocks Mountain Guides in Seneca Rocks, West Virginia, for writing the compelling foreword for *Peak Experiences*. Tom is a prolific first ascentionist with FA's all over the world but especially in Thailand and West Virginia. He is also a major contributor to John Long's definitive "How to Rock Climb" as well as Long's treatise on climbing anchors. I was introduced to him by a mutual friend early in my climbing "career" and took my first trad climbing class from one of his guides at Seneca Rocks. Tom and his guides were always very kind and welcoming to my son Austin and asked about him when he wasn't with me. For those interested in exploring the sport of rock climbing or expanding their skills, I can't think of a better place to go than Seneca Rocks Mountain Guides.

Finally, I'd like to dedicate this book to my son Austin. He has been my primary and most beloved climbing partner for 14 years. He is all that anyone could ask of a son, friend and partner. My life has been in his hands and his in mine many times, and there is no one I would trust more with such a shared responsibility.

To all climbers – current and future: Climb safe and explore the edges of your comfort zone!

Leading an ordinary middle class American existence, a happenchance party transforms a preordained mundane existence. Fighting age, conditioning and weight, the next 14 years inexorably leads the author to question his sanity as he huddles in a tent at 19,620 feet deciding if he should continue up the highest peak in the Americas. This is the story of what happens when one decides to find a little more in life.

William J. Trainor, Jr., Ph.D., CFA, is a Professor of Finance in the Department of Economics and Finance at East Tennessee State University. Dr. Trainor has published extensively in journals such as Financial Review, Journal of Index Investing, Journal of Personal Finance, Journal of Financial Planning, Journal of Investing and Financial Services Review, among others. In 2012, he received ETSU's School of Business and Technology's Faculty Excellence Award for Scholarship. Bill is an avid runner, mountain biker and semi-retired climber. When not in the classroom or doing research, he can usually be found in the woods or on a rock.

Manson has written a tale of personal and family adventure that will appeal to climbers and armchair adventurers alike. His climbing journey, both alone and with his son, comes alive in his text and pictures. - Eric J. Hörst

Eric Hörst is an internationally recognized climber, performance coach, and author. He has established over 400 first ascents and authored eight books, including the classics Training for Climbing, How to Climb 5.12, and Maximum Climbing.

Climbing did more for me than a typical sport could. It helped form a strong bond between my father and me and provided inspiration and motivation. This story shows how that passion ignited and developed in both of us and, for me, launched a committed and rewarding climbing career. - Austin Boze

Austin Boze, the author's son, qualified for and competed in nine consecutive sport climbing youth national championships and won one of them. As an undergraduate college student, climbing is still a big part of his life. He is grateful for the role climbing played in the evolution of his relationship with his dad.

Peak Experiences is a book about the power of the mountains and the transformational journey they provided in the life of Manson Boze. It is also the story of how those mountains helped form a connection between a father and his son. It is a story many climbers can relate to but the non-climbing world may find difficult to understand - about the internal journey and external struggles that the high and wild places of the world lead many of us down. It is the reason why, at odds with what most people see as logical, sane behavior, we travel to these places time and time again despite the cost - monetary, physical, and psychological. Whether we summit or not, whether we push through a move or back down, and even if we fall, we never really fail because we make deep connections with our partners and the mountains, and we learn about ourselves along the way. - Coop Cooperstein

Mike "Coop" Cooperstein is the owner of Montana Alpine Guides and Andes Mountain Guides. He is a consummate adventurer and climber. He has a master's degree in Earth Science from Montana State University and has guided clients up some of the most difficult mountains and to some of the most remote places on earth for more than 17 years. During the few months of the year he is not traveling or working in the mountains, he resides in Bozeman, Montana.

About the Author

$\mathcal{M}$anson Boze was 56 when he traveled to Argentina to attempt a guided ascent of Aconcagua - the second tallest of the "seven summits" - the tallest mountain on each of the seven continents. He was 13 years into an amateur climbing career that began at the not-so-young age of 43. Manson had a demanding 20 year career with a Fortune 50 corporation that started in Richmond, VA and took him to Charlotte, NC and New York City before returning to Richmond, followed by 10 years as an executive at a small non-profit.

He started climbing in the (then) brand new climbing gym in Richmond with his 6 year old son. They both fell in love with the sport and explored many of its styles and variations. He'll be the first to tell you that he is at best an intermediate rock climber and only dabbles at the edges of mountaineering - the exploration of serious mountains with their many challenges and risks. While climbing and related endeavors may not be for everyone, Manson writes to share that some version of the sport may offer incredible opportunities for many. From relatively safe/tame* climbing in the climate controlled environs of the local climbing gym to wrestling with tall cliffs, glaciers, altitude, temperature extremes and remote settings, there's an aspect of climbing that will appeal to most athletically inclined and adventurous individuals. It can also be a fantastic family outing and a venue for sharing experiences with one's kids - as it was for Manson.

Manson's son Austin, now a college student, competed in nine consecutive youth national championships in competitive climbing and still rock climbs at a very high level today. Their experience sharing a rope over the course of Austin's developmental years helped forge a special bond between father and son.

*Climbing in any environment can be dangerous and entails risk of injury or death.

Prologue

Argentina - Aconcagua High Camp
19,620 feet above sea level
January 17, 2012

At 19,620' Camp Colera is the highest campsite on the highest mountain in the world outside of Asia - Aconcagua. That makes Aconcagua the second highest of the so called seven summits – the tallest summit on each of the seven continents. That sounds like a major distinction – and it is – but it doesn't seem quite as impressive when we learn that it ranks somewhere around 400th among all of the mountains of the world. That's because there are about 400 higher summits in Asia – spread among the Karakoram and Himalaya ranges. They include Everest - at 29,029 feet, the tallest mountain in the world. I say "about" 400 higher summits because these things really aren't that precise. First, there is a fair amount of uncertainty regarding the precise height (above sea level) of the summits of many mountains. Second, there are a variety of ways to determine whether a peak is a stand-alone summit or a sub-peak of another mountain. The summit of Aconcagua stands at 22,841 feet above sea level – plenty high to challenge a fit person but nowhere near as technically challenging as many other high peaks. Camp Colera sits on a shoulder of the mountain at 19,620 feet – some 3,000 feet below the summit. That's where I was in January, 2012 when I decided to write this book.

LEFT Aconcagua - taken from Bonete

PEAK EXPERIENCES

There are libraries full of books written by serious mountaineers and rock climbers about their exploits on the world's many challenging mountains and cliffs and the variety of routes that ascend their flanks. To be clear, I don't consider myself a serious mountaineer or a rock climber of any acclaim, in fact I didn't even start climbing until I was 43 years old - and that was mostly in the local climbing gym. I didn't reach the summit of a "fourteener[1]" until I was 46 years old. I am at best an intermediate level climber and mostly an armchair mountaineer[2]. But I find the grandeur, scope and challenges – physical, intellectual and psychological – associated with mountains compelling, in fact irresistible. So why would someone who has no credible resume of alpine accomplishments presume to write a book? One of the reasons is to share that one needn't be a world class athlete, a sponsored climber or a crazy risk-taker to explore the mountains. That said, fitness matters and it is important to acquire some (easily learned) skills and to develop the ability to assess risk and the discipline to act upon one's assessments. I also suspect that there are a lot of people who can relate to my situation – a regular guy who worked a regular job (until I recently retired), lived in a regular (non-mountainous) place, raised a regular family

---

1 A fourteener is a mountain whose summit is at least 14,000 feet above sea level. There are a number of them in the 48 contiguous states of the US. The tallest is Mt. Whitney in California at 14,505'. By far the largest concentration is found in Colorado where there are over 50 such summits.

2 Rock climbing is sometimes considered a sub-set of mountaineering – a sport within a sport. It generally entails climbing steep cliffs and artificial climbing walls. Mountaineering generally entails forays into the mountains, often for multiple days or weeks, with exposure to a variety of terrain including trails, rock, and snow and ice, often miles from civilization and at elevations and in conditions where timely rescue may not be a possibility.

and lived a regular life – who happens to have a lust for adventure and exploration. This book is written primarily for such people. This is also a story of how climbing provided a venue for the development of a wonderful relationship between me and my son.

I had struggled mightily to reach Camp Colera from our previous camp, Nido de Condores (18,270'). I was in great shape – at least for a guy my age - so gaining a thousand feet or so of elevation over the course of a mile or so would have been no big deal – at least not at sea level. The problem is the higher one goes, the less air there is to breathe – literally. Air pressure at sea level is about 14.7 pounds per square inch (psi). At 18,000' air pressure is 7.34 psi – about half the sea level pressure. It isn't hard to imagine how this might affect the human body. Despite my overall fitness and successful acclimatization I found myself taking 2 to 3 breaths for each step on the steeper sections of the snow covered slope. It took me over three hours to cover the short distance.

Acclimatization is the process of adjusting one's body to the thinner air found at higher altitude. It is accomplished by gaining altitude rather slowly while the body literally adjusts its physiology – producing more and larger red blood cells. The rule of thumb is to average no more than 1,000 feet per day once beyond eight or ten thousand feet. It can also help to climb high during the day – to ferry loads to higher camps for example – then return to the previous camp to sleep. Failure to acclimatize properly can result in discomfort, disability or even death. There are three common maladies associated with altitude. The first and most benign is acute mountain sickness or AMS. Symptoms include dizziness or light-headedness, fatigue, headache, nausea or vomiting, loss of appetite, difficulty sleeping, rapid pulse and shortness of breath (with exertion). AMS can usually be resolved fairly quickly by descending. A thousand feet or so will often do the trick. Much more serious are high altitude pulmonary edema (HAPE) and high altitude cerebral edema (HACE), both of which can lead to death if not addressed promptly with the onset of symptoms. There are ample resources on these ailments so I will not belabor them here.

In addition to proper acclimatization there are medications that can help prevent and/or alleviate altitude related illness. The most common are Diamox (acetazolamide) and Dexamethasone. Be sure to consult a physician who is versed in altitude issues and get input from experienced mountaineers before using these medications, especially Dexamethasone.

I had signed on with a guide service - Andes Mountain Guides (AMG) - for one of their expeditions to the summit of Aconcagua. Starting at the park entrance at about 9,000 feet, we had spent twelve days working our way up the mountain. Some of those days were long and grueling but others were rest days. Our guides, Mike "Coop" Cooperstein and Leo Rasnik, had planned our ascent to provide ample time to acclimatize. Stops along the way included Confluencia Camp at 11,090', a way station with a variety of services including catered meals and toilet facilities provided by several expedition services, and Plaza de Mulas Camp at 14,340' which serves as base camp for

Aconcagua. Plaza de Mulas or Mulas for short is a bustling little settlement during the Aconcagua climbing season which starts in December and runs through February. The expedition services offer meals, tents, toilets and even hot showers to weary climbers. There is even an art gallery and a bar at base camp! At any given time during the climbing season there are probably several hundred people at Plaza de Mulas.

As you might have guessed Plaza de Mulas translates to Plaza of Mules. The name derives from the fact that base camp is the end of the road for the daily mule trains that cover the twenty odd miles from the park entrance to Mulas. The mountain is too steep and snow covered above Mulas for the mules to safely carry loads. Most climbers use the mules to carry their mountaineering gear, food and other supplies to base camp. Arrangements are made though the expedition services. Above base camp climbers can hire porters to carry loads from camp to camp. Porters can also be secured through the expedition services. Most of the expedition services, which are granted concessions each year by the park service, also provide guide services – but not all of the guide services are affiliated with an expedition service.

AMG contracted with Inca Expedition Service. They hauled all of our group gear (tents, food, etc.) to Confluencia and Plaza de Mulas via mule train and further up the mountain via porter. The mule trains are guided by gauchos – Spanish for cowboy. Hikers move out of their way as they gallop up and down the trail with surprising speed and agility. The porters who operate above base camp

xix

Mule Team Arrives at Aconcagua Base Camp

are even more remarkable. They carry loads exceeding 20 kilograms (about 44 pounds) at astonishing speeds up and down the mountain. On Aconcagua the porters do not travel with their clients – or even spend the night up high on the mountain. They start and end each day back at base camp. Most climbing parties camp at three locations above base camp. There are several to choose from. Our camp 1 was Camp Canada at 16,570'. Our camp 2 was Nido de Condores at 18,270'. And our camp 3 was Camp Colera at 19,620'. Porters start out at base camp each morning, carry a load to camp 1, pick up a new load to carry to camp 2 where they pick up a new load to carry to camp 3 then repeat the process on the way down – or carry directly from camp 3 to base camp since most parties descend all the way from their high camp to base camp in one long (and quad-busting) day. These guys (and they are all guys – at least as far as I could see) must be among the most fit human beings on earth!

On Aconcagua, clients of guided expeditions (and unguided climbers) can elect to hire porters to carry their personal loads or to carry it all themselves. A fully loaded mountaineering pack can easily exceed 50 pounds and loads north of 60 pounds are not at all uncommon. For that reason most parties "ferry" loads from camp to camp – or hire porters. Some do a combination of both as we did. Ferrying loads just means carrying gear to the next camp and returning to sleep at the previous camp. Fitness is obviously important to a successful expedition. Most climbers start training months before their trips.

Climbing style varies from mountain to mountain, country to country and continent to continent. Porters are rare to non-existent in the United States even on the tallest US summit – Denali (aka Mt. McKinley) in Alaska. On Denali climbers typically arrive on the mountain by bush plane. Most have bulging packs exceeding 50 pounds and more gear loaded onto a sled which they tow behind them. In the Himalaya, Sherpas (which is really an ethnicity) serve as porters but most people simply call them Sherpas. The terms have almost become interchangeable. On another popular summit, Kilimanjaro in Tanzania on the African continent, porters travel up the mountain with their clients (actually ahead of their clients) and set up each camp with toilet and dining tents in addition to sleeping tents. They also cook for their clients.

Back on Aconcagua at high camp on summit day - the temperature was 4 degrees Fahrenheit at 4:00 AM when

Coop called out for the team to get up and start preparing for our summit attempt. I was already awake. In fact I had been awake pretty much all night. It is very hard to sleep at altitude. Some people can't sleep at all and others piece together restless naps. There are several reasons for the phenomenon but they all have to do with the lack of air – and therefore oxygen. Compound the physiological challenge with the anxiety associated with climbing high on cold and dangerous mountains and not many people enjoy a good night's sleep the night before summit day. I had been tossing and turning in my down sleeping bag since I doused my headlamp around 10:00 the night before. I was fairly comfortable despite being in a nylon tent which was pitched on a snowfield. Modern backcountry equipment is remarkably effective. My two sleeping pads – a bottom layer of closed cell foam topped by a thin inflatable air mattress – insulated me from the cold snow below and my 850 fill down bag – rated for up to minus 20 degrees – made the single digit temps quite bearable.

My thoughts during the night revolved around whether or not I was even going to attempt the summit.

Peak Experiences Indoor Rock Climbing Gym

Chapter 1

In the Beginning

Richmond, Virginia
Fall, 1998 – Spring, 2000

*I*n the fall of 1998 I had been separated for about a year and was renting a room in a condo from another single guy. It was far from an ideal housing arrangement, especially on weekends that I had my son, Austin who was about to turn 6 years old. Since I was still paying for most of the expenses associated with the house I owned with my wife and since I was out of work at the time there were not many alternatives. Every opportunity to get out of that condo and away from town was welcome. Austin and I often took day trips to the mountains or the beach or just went for walks in the park. One weekend he was invited to a birthday party which was being held at the brand new local rock climbing gym - Peak Experiences Indoor Climbing Gym. I had never even heard of a rock climbing gym so I was curious to see what it was all about. I had been a pretty athletic and "outdoorsy" guy most of my life – from Boy Scouting days in my early teens to crewing on racing sailboats in my 20's and 30's and owning my own boats at times to hiking in the mountains of Virginia. I started skiing as a child and took several trips to ski at the fantastic resorts in Colorado over

1

the years. While there were multi-year gaps in my devotion to fitness, most years I ran 3 to 5 miles fairly regularly and often did calisthenics. I had even gotten into rappelling[1] off of cliffs at one point. But I had never rock climbed – and frankly I wasn't in very good shape at the time.

    While Austin participated in the birthday party festivities, I struck up a conversation with the staff and toured the gym. The staff members were terrific young folks who were clearly psyched to be doing what they were doing. They offered to let me try a few climbs while they belayed[2] me. I was instantly hooked. The combination of physical and mental challenge and fear management were like none I had ever experienced before. I found myself hoping that Austin was enjoying it as much as I was. You probably would not be reading this book if he hadn't. That day marked a turning point in both of our lives and opened the avenue by which our bond grew exponentially over the years.

    After the party I asked Austin how he liked it. "Awesome" was his reply. I asked if he'd like to do more of it and he said "definitely." We both beamed from ear to ear. I returned the next day to take the "Learn the Ropes" class which is where one learns to belay, along with other important information to climb safely in the climbing gym. Before I left, I bought a few books about climbing from their gear shop. The next weekend we were back in the gym. Austin was too young to belay me at first but there was of-

---

1 Rappelling is lowering one's self down a steep cliff by sliding down a rope – usually using a rappel or belay/rappel device.

2 To belay is to tend the rope the climber is attached to. The belayer feeds out or takes in rope as the situation demands as the climber climbs. The objective is to minimize the distance and impact of a fall should one occur.

ten someone on the gym staff or another friendly climber willing to lend a hand. From the start, we could be found at the gym two or three times a week, sometimes more. Before long, we knew everyone who worked there and many of the regular climbers. Within months we had subscribed to all of the climbing magazines and had started to acquire gear. Like many sports, climbing has its own array of gear and its own lingo. Harnesses and ropes may be familiar to just about everyone but some of the gear would be unrecognizable to most people. We both started to make friends in the climbing community, many of whom are still among our closest friends.

One friend in particular played a key role in expanding our climbing horizons. I met Bill in the gym and we hit it off quickly. We both have libertarian leanings and to say that we are not very religious would be an understatement. We are both pretty opinionated and it turned out that many of our opinions were the same or similar. Bill had climbed all over the United States and had even done some climbing abroad. He's about 10 years younger than me but he didn't seem to mind taking an aging (and slightly overweight) neophyte under his wing and he and Austin hit it off as well. The closest really good climbing to Richmond is in West Virginia – a three to four hour drive away. The two best known and most popular climbing destinations in West Virginia are the New River Gorge, just north of Beckley, WV, and Seneca Rocks, which is about 60 miles west of Harrisonburg, Virginia. It wasn't long before we were going there on a fairly regular basis with Bill and others that we met in the gym. Austin came on many but not all of these trips.

PEAK EXPERIENCES

By the spring of 1999 I had gotten a good job with the Greater Richmond Chamber of Commerce as their VP of Administration with responsibility for Finance, HR, Facilities, IT and Legal – kind of a big fish in a small pond. I really didn't expect to be there more than a year or two but I loved it there and ended up staying for ten years. About the same time I got an apartment of my own – right across the street from the climbing gym. Austin now had his own room (in my home – he already had his own room in his mother's house). It was a positive step for both of us.

We had been climbing for about a year when I decided that it was time for Austin to learn to belay. At seven he was still too young to belay in the gym so I taught him outdoors. Our size difference was pretty dramatic so it was important to anchor him to the ground so that if/when I fell he would not go flying into the air. We also used an auto-locking belay device called a Gri-Gri which is made by a French company called Petzyl. A belay device is a contraption that attaches to the belayer's harness and through which the rope passes. It makes it possible to stop the rope when the climber falls. This is called arresting a fall. Climbers more commonly call it "catching" a fall. When a Gri-Gri is suddenly loaded its spring loaded cam automatically locks down on the rope – with little effort from the belayer. Many consider them to be safer than less expensive traditional belay devices which require a bit more attention from the belayer. This device also made it relatively easy for Austin to lower me back down from the top of a climb. With him anchored to the ground and with this belay device all he had to do was operate the belay device. Strength and weight were taken out of the equation.

IN THE BEGINNING

As Austin got a little taller, his climbing skills improved rapidly. He was among the youngest regular climbers in the gym and he had quite a following. When he was on the wall he'd frequently get words of encouragement from nearby climbers. It seemed that everyone knew his name. In fact for years when I met someone new in the gym, they would say "oh, you're Austin's dad." After a while I just started introducing myself that way. By then, Peak Experiences had formed a youth climbing team that was competing against other gyms up and down the east coast and across the country. There was even a governing body for the sport which at the time was called the Junior Climbing Competition Association – JCCA. The organization has morphed and merged with other "competing" organizations over the years – and become far more professional. It is now the sanctioning body for all competition climbing in the US and goes by the name USA Climbing. It is headquartered in Boulder, Colorado. At first I resisted the efforts of the coach of the "junior team" as it was called to recruit Austin. He was probably two years younger than the youngest kid then on the team and frankly I didn't want to ruin a good thing by turning it into a competition. I did take him to a couple of competitions though in the spring of 2000 – as an independent climber. The youngest age category in competition climbing is 11 and under. Austin was 7. He did pretty well considering his age and size. I think he even got one third place finish. We talked it over at length and I agreed to let him join the team for the season that would begin in January, 2001. Training would begin in September, 2000.

Austin and Bill on a belay ledge in Boulder Canyon - Summer 2000

Chapter 2

Our First Big Climbing Trip

Boulder, Colorado
July, 2000

As the summer of 2000 approached I wanted to expand our climbing horizons and set out on an adventure. Our friend Bill was thinking of traveling out west to climb in the Rockies and planned to take his dad along. We agreed to join forces. My ex-wife – Austin's mom – asked if she could come along. We agreed. Bill and I hoped to do some climbing that would be a little out of Austin's range at that age and it would be nice to have her along so that they could do other things while we climbed. Her one condition was that she would not sleep in a tent so I rented a small pop-up camper. It was a bit of a nuisance towing a trailer but it was a comfy place to sleep and it was even air-conditioned. Bill and his dad left several days before us. They also towed a camper that his dad owned. Once we met up with them in Colorado we were quite the caravan on the highways of Colorado and Wyoming.

Austin's mom doesn't climb. In fact she really doesn't do anything "outdoorsy" or athletic. She was a good sport though on this trip and even "hiked" in to watch us climb on some of the shorter approaches. On days that Austin didn't climb the two of them explored the nearby sights.

Our first stop was Boulder, Colorado. I had mixed feelings about Boulder at first but over the years I would come to love the place – and Austin would eventually choose the University of Colorado (at Boulder) for college. As I write this Boulder is on a short list of places in the Rocky Mountain West that I am considering moving to. There really aren't many camping options in the vicinity of Boulder so we set up at an inn that offers limited camping

Our camper parked near Boulder, Austin's Mom in the background

several miles up Boulder Canyon from the city of Boulder. We had driven straight through to Boulder from Richmond with stops only for gas and food so we were pretty beat. That would be the first of quite a few drives between Richmond and Boulder that I would take – some of them solo – over the course of the next decade or so. A good night's rest was all we needed to be ready to climb the next day. We slept late – maybe 8:00 or so. I prepared breakfast for the crew and then Austin, Bill and I took a driving tour of Boulder Canyon. We picked a dramatic cliff on the opposite side of Boulder Creek from the road and parked in a pull-off. In order to cross the creek we had to perform a Tyrolean Traverse – an exciting first for Austin and me. A Tyrolean Traverse requires attaching yourself to a rope or wire strung tightly between two points on opposite sides of the obstacle using a carabiner or pulley and pulling yourself across the void.

    We climbed several classic trad routes on the dramatic cliff, high above Boulder Canyon, Boulder Creek and the roadway. Trad is short for traditional. There are two basic systems to "protect" climbers from long falls when rock climbing. The traditional or trad method uses temporary gear such a runners (loops of strong webbing), carabiners and a variety of odd-looking items and devices that fit in cracks and crevices in the rock and to which the climber attaches his rope. These items include "nuts," "chocks," "hexes" and "cams." The idea is that, though relatively easy to insert in (and remove from) a crack from one direction, they are unlikely to come out in the direction they will be pulled (generally downward) in the event of a fall. Usually the last person on the team to climb "cleans" the gear and the party leaves the route exactly as they found it. The other system – called sport climbing – involves bolting a piece of metal to the wall using expansion bolts (preferably stainless steel). The piece of metal is called a hanger and it has a hole large enough to accommodate a carabiner, which is hung from the hanger as the climber ascends the route and to which the climber attaches his rope. This obviously requires that holes be drilled into the rock. The bolt and the hanger become permanent and are available for subsequent parties to use.

While trad climbing has been around the longest, sport climbing began in the 1970's and increased in popularity in the 1980's and 1990's. During the 1990's there was much debate in the climbing community over the "ethics" of climbing and related protection systems. The debate has mostly subsided today with a general agreement that routes that are reasonably protected with trad (temporary) gear should not be bolted – though there are certainly some exceptions. There are also many places (including most national parks) where bolting is no longer allowed – or is subject to strict limitations. There are undoubtedly far more sport climbers today than trad climbers. Sport climbing requires much less gear (to climb routes that are already bolted) and is considered by many to be safer than trad climbing. I enjoy both. Austin prefers sport climbing. Most folks are willing to try more difficult climbs (with the associated greater likelihood of falling) when bolted protection is available than they are on traditional routes.

The next day we ventured to El Dorado Canyon – about 5 miles south of Boulder where the three of us climbed Bastille Crack – a super-classic three pitch[1] route with moderate difficulty. We considered it to be quite an accomplishment for a 7 year old! As an added bonus the route starts right next to the road that passes through the

---

1 A pitch is a section of a (longer – "multi-pitch") climbing route – the territory between one belay station and the next – often defined by the length of the rope and/or the terrain of the route.

canyon and Austin's mom was able to set up a portable chaise and watch her son climb an awesome route that topped out about 300 feet above the road. She had seen him climb short routes outdoors once or twice before but that was the first major outdoor route she saw him climb. We had a terrific group dinner that night at one of the fine restaurants on the Pearl Street Mall in Boulder to celebrate our success.

The next day we set our sights on the Third Flatiron. If you've been to Boulder, Colorado you have seen the Flatirons. They are the monstrous brown rocks protruding from the earth just south and west of town. The First Flatiron towers over the campus of the University of Colorado. The east faces of the first three Flatirons are shaped roughly like the bottom on an iron – the kind we iron clothes with. They are steep and tall – about 1,000 feet – but not quite vertical. This was going to be a longer day of climbing so Austin opted out but he and his mom hiked

Austin and his Mom (in background) on the path to the Flatirons

part of the way on the approach trail with us. We got to the base of the climb a little later than we had hoped – probably around 11:00 AM. The first pitch was a variation from the standard route. Bill chose it because it was more technically difficult than anything we had done together. After climbing relatively easy (for him) routes that were within Austin's and my range, he wanted for more of a challenge. I think he got what he was looking for – and I know I did. I won't belabor my efforts to surmount the crux of the pitch but Bill has used the term belly flop to describe it. It wasn't pretty. I've sometimes considered going back to that pitch to see if my improved skills would have any impact.

While the Flatirons are spectacular, both from the ground along the Front Range and from the perspective of the climber perched on their flanks, they are dark colored and face east so they are warmed (heated) by the sun coming up in the east. On warm, sunny, windless days it can get pretty hot up there. We were pretty well roasted by the time we reached the summit and prepared to rappel off the back side of the formation. Bill actually coaxed me into leading the last pitch of the route (which was quite easy but also quite high up). It was my first lead on trad gear and I was thrilled. Our spirits were high but we had consumed all of the water we had brought along with us. We were eager to get back to our packs at the base of the climb and from there back to the parking lot where we had a cooler full of liquids. The back side of the Third Flatiron is overhung, meaning it is more than vertical. That makes the 200 foot rappel quite exciting because the climber is hanging in the air from his rope and has no direct contact with the rock for most of the way down to the ground. It was by far the longest free hanging rappel I had ever done. The day was shaping up to be the highlight of my climbing career thus far.

We racked our gear on our harnesses and coiled the ropes over our backs. We did not bring any shoes besides the somewhat uncomfortable climbing shoes on our feet. Our approach shoes were back at our packs. The descent trail was not supposed to be very long or very difficult – or so the guidebook, which we had left at our packs, said. I wasn't to find out that is true until years later (summer of 2011) when I next climbed the Third Flatiron. Bill had reviewed the details of the route and descent in the guidebook before we started climbing and concluded that the descent would be "obvious." He pointed south and said "that looks like the trail." In reality the descent trail goes around the north side of the Third Flatiron. The first part of our hike out involved some fairly steep but non-technical rock scrambling interspersed with what could pass as trail. After a while we found ourselves in an overgrown gully – full of briars and deadfall. It was a miserable and painful obstacle course – and the sun continued to beat down on us. We were both dehydrated. Eventually we reached a point where we could move back to the north and skirt the base of the Third Flatiron but by now we were back in the woods so it was difficult to get our bearings and know our exact location. My feet were in quite a bit of pain from hiking in climbing shoes – something they absolutely are not intended for. My hamstrings and calves were starting to cramp. I don't recall how long we hiked but I do remember that it felt like hours. In reality it was probably only an hour or so.

Finally we were able to start moving uphill again toward our packs but I couldn't make it. My legs were cramping to the point where I was balled up in the fetal position on the ground trying to stretch out the cramps. It was quite painful. At least it was getting late in the afternoon and the sun had now moved behind the Third Flatiron. We were in the shade. After offering a fair amount of useless advice and getting some entertainment from my predicament, Bill headed off to get some water. We weren't sure if we had left any in our packs so he was going to check there first then go to the parking lot and back if he had no luck at the packs. Another chunk of time passed by as the cramps slowly subsided. Eventually I could get up and move. I very slowly made my way back to my pack which I shouldered and headed down the trail toward the parking lot. Bill had taken his pack with him. I figured I would run into him as he made his way back up the trail with the water.

After a while I found myself back at the parking lot. There was no sign of Bill. First things first - I drank a couple of bottles of sports drink then wandered over to the map on the trailhead kiosk. It turns out there are a couple of different trails that lead to the Third Flatiron. Bill had taken an alternate trail – for variety he later said. After a while he re-appeared at the parking lot having not found me where he left me. It had been a long day. The climbing had been fantastic but, while it didn't rise to the level of "epic," the hike out was definitely a "learning experience." I learned there's more to climbing bigger routes than the trip up the rock. I also learned to double-check behind Bill whenever he says "it'll be obvious" or "that looks like the way." It turns out he is well known among his climbing buddies for the first of those expressions. Climbers love to joke around at one another's expense and my relationship with Bill is no exception, but at the end of the day he is among my closest friends. We can go a year or more without seeing or talking to one another and pick right up where we left off the last time we were together.

The author with the diamond face and summit of Long's Peak in the background

Chapter 3

Into the Rockies

Estes Park, Colorado
July, 2000

*T*he next day we were off to Estes Park, gateway to Rocky Mountain National Park. RMNP is not as well-known as some of the other national parks but it is as spectacular as any. We got campsites in an RV park next to Mary's Lake and spent the next few days climbing at lower elevations, including Lumpy Ridge. We toured the park by car and spent a few days climbing in the Lumpy Ridge section of the park. There was much discussion of whether or not to try the hike up Long's Peak, the park's high point and one of Colorado's famed 14,000 foot summits. They call them 14-ers and there are

Austin with the Twin Owls (Lumpy Ridge) in the background

over 50 of them in the state – far more than any other state. We elected to try it on our last day in Estes. Our party consisted of Bill, his dad and me. Austin and his mom would take in the sights in Estes that day.

    From the Long's Peak trailhead parking lot we could see a sky choked with stars. But once we stepped into the woods there was nothing but inky black. The light from our headlamps darted here and there as we adjusted our boots, packs and trekking poles. It was 3:30 in the morning – dark and cool, probably in the mid-50's. We had crawled out of our bunks about a half hour earlier at the nearby campground and quietly dressed for a long day on the mountain. We had prepared our packs and gear the night before so that we wouldn't make too much noise and wake up Austin and his mom.

    The summit of Long's Peak sits at 14,255 feet above sea level. The trailhead elevation is at 9,400' so climbing it entails nearly 5,000 feet of elevation change – in each direction. To make it a bit more interesting the distance from the trailhead to the summit and back is about 15 miles. As Bill told me many times: "It's not trivial." Bill is well known for pulling the legs of his partners but about this he wasn't kidding. I had been hiking around my home state of Virginia since my Boy Scout days in the 1960's, including many of the peaks in our well known Blue Ridge Mountains and in Shenandoah National Park. The high point in Virginia though is 5,729 foot tall Mount Rogers in the southwestern part of the state. To say that I had no meaningful frame of reference is an understatement.

    I had questioned Bill on why we needed to start out so early in the morning – something he called an "alpine start." That's a term I would become very familiar with and an activity I would come to love over the coming years. It is possible to camp in an area called The Boulderfield high on the flanks of Longs Peak at an elevation of 12,760, breaking the ascent into a two day affair, but most people who are doing the standard route do it in a day. Summertime in the Rockies brings afternoon thunderstorms on a nearly daily basis. They generally sweep through between 1:00 and 5:00 in the afternoon but earlier and later storms are not uncommon. Lightning from these storms pummels the high peaks. Hence it is wise to attain and retreat from the exposed summits of these mountains before the storms arrive. The rule of thumb is to retreat if it becomes clear that you will not summit by noon – earlier if approaching weather (generally from the west) threatens. That's one of the main reasons alpine starts are common in the Rockies. Also, some of the longer hikes/climbs can take 12 hours or more roundtrip so if you want to be back for dinner you have to start early.

There were only a few cars in the parking lot as we signed the trailhead register and marched into the woods. I was excited but nervous. I had no idea what to expect. In the days before we had done some rock climbing on Lumpy Ridge – a row of granite "lumps" that preside over a drainage near the entrance to Rock Mountain National Park (RMNP). Their summits are about 1,000 feet above the valley floor and the approaches from the parking lot are pretty moderate – ranging from 15 minutes to an hour or so. Lumpy Ridge offers spectacular views of Longs Peak and the other high peaks that stride the continental divide in RMNP. Longs is imposing – noticeably taller than anything else around with steep rocky sides and a rounded summit that towers way above treeline. From that perspective it is not readily apparent how one can gain the summit without some technical and dangerous climbing. In fact there are numerous routes up Longs, most of which are technical (require specialized climbing gear and skills) and challenging. The most traveled route, called The Keyhole route can on the other hand be climbed by anyone with adequate fitness and stamina once the winter snow melts off – usually by early July. Those with a fear of heights will find the upper sections of the mountain daunting though as one must traverse very exposed ledges with steep drop-offs approaching 1,000 feet.

    As we moved along all I could really see was whatever happened to be lit by the beam of my headlamp – usually the little patch of trail in front of me, occasionally Bill's boots on the trail ahead of me. We talked little, taking in the solemn quiet of the surrounding forest and the sound of the mountain stream that the trail followed up the flanks of the mountain. The main Longs Peak trail is well worn and well maintained. After a while we stopped for a rest and a snack. It was still dark. We had only seen one other party on the mountain – a pair who breezed past us as if we were standing still. Bill is a runner and he's extremely competitive. He didn't like being passed. He decided to pick up the pace and leave me and his dad to our own devices. We decided to all proceed at our own pace and meet up later somewhere on the mountain. Both Bill and I had FRS radios – walkie-talkies - but despite numerous efforts we were never able to make contact with one another. As Bill zoomed off ahead of me I gradually pulled away from his dad – eventually I was completely isolated. I felt as though

I had the entire massive mountain to myself. While this was daunting it was also exhilarating.

    The Rockies are home to lots of bears – mountain lions too. Mountain lions are rarely seen though and even more rarely attack humans. Bears, on the other hand, do occasionally attack, particularly when they are surprised or feel threatened or when they feel that their cubs are in danger. The worst place a hiker can possibly be is between a momma bear and her cubs. When traveling along a trail in bear country with limited visibility – either due to darkness, foliage or topography – experienced hikers make noise so as not to surprise a bear. Usually if they hear you coming they will move aside and the hiker never even sees them. They are no more eager for encounters with us than we are with them. Some people sing, others whistle, some yodel and others clap their hands. Some even attach bells to their trekking poles. I generally click my trekking poles together loudly every few minutes, especially in the dark.

    I was keenly aware of the possibility of a bear encounter as I cruised along the trail alone that morning in the dark. Fortunately that didn't happen. I did however see a pair of expensive sunglasses sitting on a rock beside the trail. They looked vaguely like Bill's sunglasses. I thought of picking them up to see if I ran into anyone looking for them on the trail but decided to leave them for their owner to find on their way back down. I later found out that they were in fact Bill's - and they were not there later that day when he returned. When we shared stories that evening he was less than happy that I had not picked them up. He had spent well over $100 on them.

It was still dark when I suddenly popped out of the trees into a clearing. There were some small scrubby pine trees and a stunted piney growth called krummholz after that but I was surprised to find that I had reached the treeline, the point at which it is too cold and/or too dry and too windy to sustain significant plant life. Treeline is at a higher elevation close to the equator and at a relatively low elevation – as low as 6,000 feet – at higher latitudes. Once again the sky became a magnificent canopy of stars with the Milky Way clearly visible. At times I found myself stopping to stare at it but I knew I had to keep moving.

As I gained altitude the light pollution from Denver and its neighboring communities along the Front Range became more and more apparent to the east and eventually the orange glow of the approaching sunrise stained the eastern sky. The rays of the rising and setting sun pass through earth's atmosphere at a shallow angle and cast a fantastic orange/gold glow on whatever light colored object they strike. It is particularly dramatic when cast upon the face of a large cliff. In the mountains this is called alpenglow. My timing was perfect to experience this phenomenon as the 3,000 foot vertical "Diamond Face" of Longs Peak came into sight. Cast in alpenglow this dramatic precipice is even more striking than its daytime appearance. I spontaneously and uncontrollably burst into tears. They were literally pouring down my face. I knew then that this would be the first of many forays into the "real" mountains. I also knew that I would have to lose weight and get in better shape if I were going to be at all proficient in alpine endeavors.

I crossed a massive boulder field (the namesake of the Boulderfield camping area) which grew steeper as I approached the ridgeline to the right of the Diamond Face of Longs and gained about another thousand feet to reach a prominent feature on the mountain called The Keyhole. It is an odd shaped break in the northern ridgeline leading to the summit of Longs. From there it is another thousand feet or so up to the summit. That's where I ran into Bill who had summited and was on the way down. He had caught up with the pair we had seen earlier and they were still together when I met him at The Keyhole. At that point I decided that I would use my remaining stamina to return to the trailhead and come back to reach the summit of Longs Peak another day. It is a good thing I did. I learned later just how hard that last thousand feet, especially given its lofty elevation, is.

Austin at the base of one of the strange rock formations at Vedawoo

Chapter 4

The Adventure Continues

Vedawoo and Jackson, Wyoming
July, 2000

$\mathcal{F}$rom Estes Park, our little caravan headed north into Wyoming. We set up camp in a fairly remote area called Vedawoo in the Medicine Bow – Routt National Forest near Laramie, Wyoming. The climbing area in Vedawoo is a bizarre collection of giant boulders, ranging in size from that of a small car to the size of a large hotel, scattered about the high plains. Some of the collection is visible from interstate 80. Camping there is purely rustic. There are no "conveniences." Because of our ambitious itinerary we only climbed in Vedawoo for a day and a half. One route stands out in my memory but I don't remember its name. Bill, by far the more experienced climber, generally selected our routes and researched the "beta"[1] in the guidebook. Early in our climbing partnership he led every pitch of every route. As I became more proficient in my climbing and my comfort with gear grew Bill taught me to lead – mostly on very easy pitches. As the second person up I was always on top rope belay and thus at very little risk of sustaining an injury if (actually when) I fell. This also made him fully re-

---

[1] Beta is the term for information about how to climb a route sometimes including recommended gear.

sponsible for routefinding (which can be quite challenging on longer routes without fixed gear[2]. Since he was the one facing all of the real challenges I usually didn't even read about the routes in the guidebook – at least not at first.

We set up our belay at the base of a fairly large chimney[3]. Bill had an enormous grin on his face as he said: "This will be fun. We will actually pass through an enclosed vertical tunnel." That did sound like fun. Little did I know. Pretty soon Bill disappeared out of sight into the "tunnel." All I could see was his rope slowly moving into the darkness. After a while Bill called out "off belay" and it was my turn. I climbed easy terrain to where the enclosure began. I looked up to see sunlight at the end of a small opening about 20 feet above me. Between me and the opening the tunnel progressively narrowed. Now and then Bill's face would appear in the opening – with the same grin. "Are you going to be able to make it?" I am considerably larger than Bill – at least in the horizontal dimension – and back then I weighed at least 20 pounds more than I do now. He has a slim runner's (and climber's) build. I look more like a (short) linebacker. He was most amused. I grunted my way up to the point that I could either have my arms above my head or down by my side but could not change positions once I committed and moved upward. My shoulders barely fit though the constriction. I struggled to get though it unaided for what seemed like an eternity – all while being subjected to Bill's unrelenting banter. Finally I had him lower

---

[2] Fixed gear is hardware permanently placed along the route such as (expansion) bolted anchors to which climbers attach their ropes to limit the magnitude of a potential fall.

[3] A chimney is a large crack-like feature in the rock bordered on at least two (and often three) sides into which a climber can fit his whole body. They can vary from quite narrow (squeeze chimneys) to quite large.

a loop of webbing down to me which I put my foot in like a stirrup. With my foot in the "stirrup" at about mid-thigh height and my arms above my head, I was able to force my body up through the hole. I was literally born again. This story has been told many times around many campfires. Since then I have made it my business to check behind Bill in the guidebook. I should have learned this lesson back in Boulder on the First Flatiron but better late than never.

From Vedawoo we crossed a large section of Wyoming to reach Jackson, Wyoming and Grand Teton National Park (GTNP) where we set up our campers in a well-appointed private campground. We spent one day checking out the tourist attractions near Jenny Lake, including the boat ride across the lake and the short hike back around the lake to the parking lot. We only had one day left before my family had to leave to get back to Virginia. Bill had decided to do a one day hike to the summit of the Middle Teton – no small undertaking. Knowing from experience that I would not be able to keep Bill's pace I agreed to drive the rest of the group on a tour of nearby Yellowstone National Park. I heard Bill start his car early that morning for his Alpine start. I wished I were going with him but I was also happy to roll over and go back to sleep. I vowed to return.

My group had a lovely day in Yellowstone. We saw Old Faithful and numerous other geothermal features, Yellowstone Falls, and a large herd of buffalo all in one day. Still I felt like I should have been in the mountains. When we met back up with Bill that night he told tales of his solo trip up the Middle Teton, including a scary encounter with a black bear and her cubs. My resolve to return grew stronger.

Chapter 5

Austin is Invited to the National Championship for the First Time

Richmond, VA
September, 2000 – Spring, 2001

*I*n September of 2000, Austin was about to turn 8. As a member of the climbing team he was granted an exception to belay in the gym. The gym is equipped with ground anchors so belaying bigger kids (or me) on toprope was not a problem. Toprope is the situation that exists when the rope is already in place when the climber starts climbing. It goes from the climber to an anchor at the top of the climb where is passes through a carabiner or other device (which acts as a pulley) and back down to the belayer at the bottom of the climb. In some situations, mostly outdoors, the belayer can be at the top of the climb. In a toprope situation falls are very short and mostly just result in the climber sitting in his harness. Injuries are rare. Despite all of that people were often surprised to see such a young person belaying others, let alone belaying me. We often found ourselves explaining the circumstances.

We continued to climb regularly through the winter of 2000/2001 and Austin began training with the team twice a week. When the competition series began in February we were eager to see how he'd stack up. We traveled to North and South Carolina, the Washington, DC area, Philadelphia and New Jersey to participate. The comps were all on Saturday mornings so we often got up very early to drive to them and returned home the same day. Once in a while we'd drive to the comp location the night before and spring for a motel room. It came as a bit of a surprise to both of us that Austin did well enough at the competitions to qualify to compete at the national championship competition which was to be held in Ann Arbor, Michigan in July. While Austin's skills had really improved it is also true that there were not many kids competing in rock climbing in those early years (early for us) – and that was particularly true on the east coast – and in the younger age categories. We elected to pass on the opportunity. Austin was disappointed but I felt like he would have gotten crushed by what I was sure were better climbers from the west coast and Rocky Mountain states. Besides he still had two more years to compete in the 11 and under category.

During that spring we traveled a few more times to West Virginia. We were gradually learning the more complicated technical aspects of climbing outdoors.

Seneca Rocks, WV with Austin waving on deck

Austin climbs at Seneca Rocks

Austin climbing at Table Rock in North Carolina

Chapter 6

Adventures Close to Home

Looking Glass, NC, Richmond, VA
Summer, 2001

We talked about going out west again in the summer of 2001 but money was a bit tight and Austin still wasn't really ready for long days in the mountains so we chose to stay closer to home. We decided to go to the mountains of North Carolina for a week or so in June along with our buddy Bill. We climbed at Table Rock and Linville Gorge, not far from Boone, and a little further south at Looking Glass, near Asheville. Looking Glass is a big granite dome – low angled on one exposure called The Nose and steep on two others. We had a great time while adding more experience to our climbing resumes.

Austin roasts marshmallows with some of his teammates on a trip to the New River Gorge

Climbing (not to mention camping) in the south during July

and August can be miserable due to the southern heat and humidity. By fall though we were headed back to West Virginia on weekends that we weren't at football games. We had acquired season tickets for University of Virginia football and become rabid fans. September also brought the beginning of a new season of climbing team and regular training sessions. Austin was about to turn 9. By now I was letting him go to the gym by himself. It was only a few hundred yards from our apartment. He had to cross one road that had very little traffic. He carried an FRS (Family Radio Service) walkie-talkie with him so that we could be in contact during the "journey." He called me from the gym when he was ready to leave to come home. That went on for a year or so until we were both comfortable with him going back and forth without the electronic tether. He spent many hours doing pull-ups and other calisthenics and working out on the campus board at the gym. A campus board is a steep fixture with hand and finger holds of various sizes and shapes. Campusing is climbing without the aid of one's feet. Since the entire body weight is born by the hands, fingers and arms it is a great upper body workout.

Chapter 7

Competitive Climbing Starts to Come Into Its Own

Richmond, VA
Early 2002

The 2002 competition season was much like the previous season but there were more kids. The sport was really starting to catch on. Competitions were often somewhat crowded – with upward of 100 kids and their parents and coaches crammed into sometimes small climbing gyms. The governing body – Junior Competition Climbing Association (JCCA) was also going through growing pains. At the time the organization was a very small non-profit based in Portland, Oregon. It had no paid staff and the volunteers who ran it were not always in synch with one another, let alone with the dozens of gym owners and coaches and hundreds of parents who made it viable. The rules were in a somewhat constant state of flux and it even seemed that they changed their name every year for about three or four years.

As I became more knowledgeable of the sport and familiar with the gyms, coaches and parents I started to volunteer to help run the comps, primarily as a belayer and judge. The competition was stiffer in 2002 and the methodology for qualifying for an invitation to the national championship changed – allowing fewer kids from our region to qualify than the previous year. As a result Austin didn't qualify that year. It was held near Portland, Oregon. He was disappointed but he had one year remaining in the 11 and under category.

Me and Austin in Rocky Mountain National Park

Chapter 8

Back to the Rockies

Estes Park, CO
July, 2002

*T*hat summer we went back to Colorado. This time it was just Austin and me. We reserved a campsite at a private campground near the entrance to Rocky Mountain National Park (RMNP) in Estes Park, Colorado for two weeks in July. We flew in to Denver with four large duffels and a cooler, stuffed to the gills with clothes and gear. Travelling by air with that much stuff can be very trying – particularly getting in and out of airports and to and from the rental car. I dreaded that part every time we did it. From the Denver airport we drove directly to Estes Park where we stocked up on groceries at the local Safeway. To save money I planned to prepare most of our meals at the campsite. I bought dry ice which kept meat, milk and cheese cold for days in our cooler. It even froze some of the items which were closer to the dry ice.

We did a fair amount of day hiking in RMNP over the course of those two weeks. We'd get up early, generally between 3:00 and 5:00 AM, eat a quick breakfast and get to our designated trailhead at or before sunrise. Most days we entered the park before the park entrance was staffed.

There were very few if any cars in the trailhead parking lots at that hour. When the gates are manned during the day and evening there is a fee to enter. I buy an annual park pass every year. The pass provides unlimited access to all national parks and most national monuments for a carload of people for a whole year. Back in 2002 they were only $50. They are still quite reasonable (for frequent park visitors) at $80.

ABOVE Austin climbs at The Monastery

BELOW Austin on "Enema Syringe"

We topped out on several of the lesser peaks and high mountain lakes in the park and became fairly familiar with the trail maps and terrain – reaching elevations of up to nearly 13,000 feet.

During those two weeks we also did a bit of technical climbing on Lumpy Ridge and a place called The Monastery. On Lumpy, I accomplished my first lead of any significance on a five pitch route named "Magical Chrome Plated Semi-Automatic Enema Syringe," a route that I had climbed with Bill two years earlier. Lead climbing is the counterpoint to climbing on toprope. When lead climbing the rope starts out on the ground with the climbers. The leader ties in to one end of the rope and attaches the rope to various pieces of protection – either bolted hangers or temporary "trad" pieces – as he climbs using carabiners and webbing. It is considerably more "engaging" than climbing on toprope. In a multi-pitch situation the second climber up the pitch is on toprope. "Enema Syringe" is not a particularly difficult route but it does have a few challenging and exposed moves and an exciting hanging belay at the end of the first pitch. A hanging belay is a belay that has no ledge to stand on. Parties at a hanging belay literally hang in their harnesses from their anchor with their feet dangling over the abyss below. We took a celebratory photo at the top – just as it began to rain a bit. I've looked back at that photo many times – partly because it was a big milestone in my climbing career – and partly because I look like a fat slob in that photo. I tried many things over the next few years to get down to a more climber-friendly weight.

Even though I was still carrying more weight than I wanted I had trained for this trip and had managed to lose a few pounds. I felt like I was in fairly decent shape and really wanted to try Longs Peak again – this time with a more favorable outcome. I was a little concerned

Austin feeling a bit "under the weather"

about Austin though. After all he was only 9. He struggled with altitude a couple of times during that week – experiencing shortness of breath, headache, and nausea, classic symptoms of acute mountain sickness. One day – toward the end of the trip – we hiked up to Spectacle Lakes. The Spectacle Lakes, at about 11,350', are shaped like a pair of "spectacles" when viewed from above and are nestled in an enormous granite cirque on the east side of Ypsilon Mountain. The scene is quite spectacular. The five mile hike in with an elevation gain of about 2,800' went smoothly – no mountain sickness. We agreed to try Longs Peak a few days later.

The night before our attempt on Longs we set the alarm for 2:30 AM. No matter how many times I do it early starts don't get any easier. It seems that either I don't get any sleep at all due to nerves and worrying about not hearing the alarm or I am rudely awakened from a deep sleep and confused about why. I do love the solitude of the trail on cool, dark mornings and, of course, the spectacular alpine environment so early starts are a fairly small price to pay. That morning we hardly spoke at all as we dressed by headlamp in our small dark tent and stumbled out into the cool night. We ate cereal bars on the way to the trailhead and arrived right on time at 3:00. I really don't remember many details from the first part of that hike for some reason. I know we weren't moving very fast because a number of people had caught up with us by the time we reached The Boulderfield at a bit over 12,000', a few hundred feet below The Keyhole feature that is the namesake of this route. There are actually pit toilets located at The Boulderfield. They seem incredibly out of place but Longs Peak is a very popular summit, partly due to its proximity to Denver and other population centers along the front range of the Rockies. The Boulderfield is also the location of the only designated campsite along this route to the summit of Longs. It's not hard to imagine the mess that might exist if the park service did not provided these toilets.

While I am on the subject of human waste I will mention that packing it out is becoming more and more the thing to do at popular backcountry locations. So called "wag bags" (they go by other names too) are available at most outdoor retailers and at some trailheads. They are essentially a double bag system with a chemical that helps to mitigate odor. On Denali (Mt. McKinley) climbers use CMC cans (clean mountain cans) – plastic cans about the size of a gallon paint can with a re-sealable top. Packing out waste is now required at a few popular backcountry destinations including Denali and The Grand Teton. These tend to be places that are too rocky, too cold or too snow covered to effectively bury it and have it biodegrade in any reasonable timeframe. It also makes sense in very popular locations where an abundance of waste would simply overwhelm the confined environment.

I remember thinking there were a lot of people tackling the Boulderfield with us but as we passed

View to the west from the Keyhole on Longs Peak

through The Keyhole (my highpoint two years earlier) and passed onto the ledges on the western side of the summit ridge there were fewer people. Many turned back at either The Boulderfield or The Keyhole. After traversing south along ledges for a ways the next obstacle is called The Trough. It is indeed a long trough or gulley – perhaps 1,000 feet long, and quite steep. It is filled with loose rocks and gravel. For just about every step up we took we slid back down about a half a step. At over 13,000' feet, compounded by the challenge of breathing the thin air, The Trough was quite frustrating. I found myself taking a breath (or two) for every step I took. Austin seemed fine – energetic even. About halfway up The Trough I told him that I didn't know if I could go any further. Austin offered encouragement and, after a rest, we plugged on. Eventually we reached the top of The Trough. It gets easier – but much more daunting – from there. First, climbers must negotiate a series of fairly narrow ledges, bounded on one side by rock wall and on the other by steep cliffs, dropping off perhaps 1,000 feet to the rocky slope below. Finally, we reached the last obstacle – and I say "final" with a taste of irony since all of these obstacles must be negotiated in reverse on the way down – The Homestretch. The Homestretch is a relatively short – perhaps 100 feet – bit of slab that leads to Longs' summit plateau. Slab in climbing parlance is steep, but not vertical, rock. This particular bit of slab has some cracks in it that provide the opportunity to wedge fingers and feet in for "traction." It looks scarier than it actually is but the consequences of a fall here would be dramatic – and terminal.

 At the summit we basked in the glory of our achievement for the better part of an hour. It was a glorious day and there was no sign of approaching thunderstorms. It was about 10:00 AM. It had taken us 7 hours to reach the summit from the trailhead. The record at the time was just over 1 hour and 18 minutes by way of a slightly shorter but more technical route. As far as I know that record still stands. In my humble opinion such feats exist only in the realm of the super-human. It took us about 4 and a half hours to get down to the trailhead. To say we were exhausted would be a massive understatement. We stopped on the way back to our campsite for a meal at our favorite diner in Estes Park – Candy's Rocky Mountaineer. Since then they have moved and now the restaurant just goes by the name The Mountaineer. It still offers good diner food though.

    We were back at our tent and ready to crash by 5:00. Austin fell asleep immediately but my mind was racing. I sat in the entryway to the tent and rehashed images of our day on the mountain – and dreamed of other bigger mountains to come. As I daydreamed I became aware of something large moving in my peripheral vision. As I forced myself back into the present and focused my eyes, it became apparent that I was watching a large black bear about 30 yards away passing by our campsite and heading toward a neighboring site. I noticed that our neighbors had left a plastic trash bag hanging from a tree about four feet off the ground. A cardinal rule in bear country is to never leave food, waste – or really anything with an odor out. It should all be secured in a bear-proof container or hung properly where it is inaccessible to bears. The neighbors were not "home" – fortunately for them.

The bear ripped open the trash bag and devoured whatever interesting leftovers he found there. Then he went over toward our neighbors' tent. I noticed that a couple at another nearby site was also watching the drama unfold from the relative safety of their minivan. I quickly woke Austin and took him over to sit with the couple in their vehicle. I went back to our campsite and grabbed a cooking pot and a spoon. Bears do not like loud noises and generally would prefer to avoid confrontations with humans. I had heard of people scaring bears off by making loud noises and standing their ground. My plan was to protect my own campsite. When I tell this story I am often told I had more bravery than brains. As I prepared the bear shredded one wall of the neighbors' tent and poked his head inside. He rooted around in there for a minute or two and eventually backed out and started ambling toward our campsite. I started beating on the pot with the spoon and slowly walked toward the bear. After what seemed like a long time (even though it was probably only a few seconds) the bear changed his angle and moved back in the direction he came from. A minute or two later it had disappeared back into the woods. It took a few minutes for the adrenalin in my system to subside. I retrieved Austin and drove back to town where we rented a hotel room for the night. It had been a big day.

Austin is crowned national champion – male 11 and under

Chapter 9

A National Champion!

Richmond, VA
Fall, 2002 – Spring, 2003

As we entered the 2002/2003 climbing season I took on more responsibilities with USA Climbing, eventually becoming the regional coordinator for the Mid-Atlantic Region, one of fifteen in the country. I scheduled and coordinated competitions at host climbing gyms in North Carolina and Virginia, scored and acted as chief judge at each of the comps. I also volunteered to help rewrite the organization's rulebook. It was a lot of work but it was also fun and rewarding. I got to know the owners and staff at many of the gyms and many of the parents. It was exciting to see the kids grow, get stronger and improve their skills from year to year.

As you might imagine, there is a fair amount of turnover among climbing gym staffs. Our gym was no exception and Austin was not thrilled with the new coaching staff at Peak. He decided to drop off of the team and compete without a team affiliation. I was to be his coach. This was his last year in the 11 and under category.

Coaching Austin proved to be a lot of fun. For the most part he was eager to work out and determined to make the most of his last year in the category. By about October of 2002 he was out-climbing me and by spring he was out-climbing most of the adults who climbed in the gym. At some point during that year Austin told a friend of ours who was in his early 40's and a very strong climber that his goal was to climb as well as him one day. Within about two years he was even out-climbing our friend. He won most of the comps he participated in that year including the regional championship. Our home gym, Peak Experiences, was on tap to host the (youth) national championship that year – an incredible incentive for Austin to do well. Austin climbed well throughout the spring season and qualified to compete in the national championship for the second time.

As the kids prepared to climb their final route at nationals Austin and two other kids were essentially tied. It was anybody's title to win. Austin climbed last. I will never forget the feeling I had when he moved successfully past the other boys' high points. I was the proudest dad in the world that day. My son was a national champion! He was ecstatic. He was awarded a plaque and an honorary invitation to join the United States Youth National Climbing Team which came with a US Team jacket and chalk bag. The US Team invitations are honorary for the two youngest age categories, 11 and under and 12/13, since those two categories do not compete at the world championship. Austin was determined to make the US Team every year – and eventually travel to a world championship. Unfortunately it was never to happen – but he wore his 2003 team jacket and chalk bag with great pride. The chalk bag hangs on the bulletin board in his room to this day.

The author, Billy and Austin topping out Irene's Arête in the Tetons. This is the photo that appeared in our local paper a few weeks later.

Chapter 10

Another Trip to the Rockies

**Jackson, Wyoming
July, 2003**

Shortly after nationals Austin and I flew to Jackson, Wyoming where we spent two weeks together in the Tetons. He was 10 years old. Our plans included a 30 mile backpacking trip along the Teton Crest Trail and a climb up The Grand Teton. For the Grand Teton I had hired a private guide through Exum Mountain Guides. One of the advantages of using guides in Grand Teton National Park and other such places is that the guide service already has climbing and camping permits for their clients so there is no gamble on climbing when you want to. An advantage of Exum in particular is their permanent high camp at the Lower Saddle of the Grand, probably the best launch pad for a summit attempt.

Exum requires clients to either take their introductory one day climbing class or do a test climb with one of their guides. Since we were somewhat experienced climbers we opted for the test climb. The day after we arrived we climbed Baxter's Pinnacle with our guide, Calvin Hebert.

Me and Calvin with (left to right) Teewinot, The Grand Teton and Mt. Owen in the background

Calvin was fairly new to Exum. I believe it was only his second summer and he was still considered a probationary guide. He was terrific though and really hit it off with Austin. He said he enjoyed climbing with kids and it showed. He was impressed by the level of Austin's climbing for his age and very supportive of his (and my) efforts.

After our day of climbing we went out for dinner, then returned to The Climber's Ranch where we were staying. The Climber's Ranch is a collection of bunkhouses run by the American Alpine Club literally at the foot of the Tetons, only a mile or so from the trailhead for Garnet Canyon, the approach to The Grand Teton and numerous other summits and climbs. Club members can stay at the ranch for only $10.00 per night. The accommodations are not luxurious but it is by far the best deal in the Jackson area. The Climber's Ranch has an outdoor bouldering wall – essentially a plywood wall about 10 feet tall covered with artificial climbing holds, just like the ones used in climbing gyms. Austin challenged Calvin to a "dual" on the climbing wall. It provided entertainment for the assembly of climbers that evening for a while until the sun started to set. Calvin prevailed but Austin gave him a contest.

The next day we got up early and headed for the trailhead at the top of the tram at Teton Village. This was the start of our four day backpacking trip along the Teton Crest Trail. We had obtained our backcountry permit from

Just off the tram, Austin is ready to go

the Jenny Lake Ranger Station two days before, just after our arrival in Jackson. While we waited for the first tram we had a leisurely breakfast at an expensive resort hotel nearby.

It was quite a contrast to our menu for the next four days in the backcountry, far from civilization.

We hiked about 8 miles into the backcountry and set up camp in an open area on a hill overlooking a small stream. We had not seen another person since leaving the trailhead at the top of the tram. There were a few nearby trees. We used one of them to hang our food out reach of bears. GTNP is home to quite a few bears – both black bears and the more fearsome grizzly bears. One of my greatest fears is being awoken by a bear snooping around my tent at night. Of course I didn't mention this to Austin. I did buy a can of bear spray – which is just very strong pepper spray – from an outfitter before we set off into the backcountry. I carried it with me everywhere we went, clipped to the hip belt on my backpack. Fortunately I never had to use it. In fact we never saw a bear on that hike.

After a lovely dinner of

Austin demonstrates proper food storage in bear country

Ramen noodles and canned chicken we watched the sun set and gazed at the stars for a bit before turning in early. The next morning we were up early for the longest segment of the backpacking trip. I had read about guided mountaineering trips in the Pacific Northwest and in Alaska. Most of the guide services recommended gaining some backpacking experience before tackling big mountains with their additional complications – like snow and ice, glaciers and crevasses. One of my goals for this trip was to increase my confidence in the backcountry. So far it was going well but the ten miles on the agenda for the day would be a good test for both of us. We covered a lot of ground that day with strikingly different landscapes. We traversed around beautiful Marion Lake on the way to the remote and somewhat desolate Death Canyon Shelf.

Death Canyon Shelf is about as far away from civilization as you can get in Grand Teton National Park. It runs along the "back" side of the park, close to Wyoming's border with Idaho. It is several miles long and bounded on one side by thousand foot tall cliffs and the other by a sheer drop of several hundred feet into Death Canyon. Its width varies from thirty or forty yards to a few hundred yards. As we approached Death Canyon Shelf, we encountered several other groups of backpackers – mostly young folks in their teens and twenties. Most were surprised to see a ten year old so far from the trailhead and offered him congratulations and words of encouragement. At the north end of the shelf we dropped down into the Alaska Basin where we set up our second campsite. Since the Alaska Basin is actually outside of the park boundary and not governed by the park service camping rules and because it sits at the confluence of several popular trails there were many people camping there. We arrived fairly late in the day so we scouted around for a while looking for a good campsite that wasn't too close to neighbors. There are numerous small lakes in Alaska Basin and we found a site on a relatively flat rock overlooking one of the lakes. I waded out into the cold water to soothe my feet which were sore from a long day of hiking with a pretty heavy pack.

    I had designs on a six day mountaineering course on Denali (aka Mt. McKinley) in Alaska the following summer and I had bought my pack with that trip in mind. It was 5,500 cubic inches (90 liters) – monstrous compared to any pack I had previously owned. I don't recall exactly what my pack weighed on that trip but I would guess around 50 pounds. I carried our tent, food, cooking kit and my clothes, sleeping bag and pad and a liter bottle of water. Austin had a small pack with an external frame to make his load a bit easier to carry. He carried only his clothes, sleeping bag and pad and a liter bottle of water. Still, it looked pretty big on him. I'd guess his pack weighed 15 pounds or so. We didn't carry a lot of water on the trail, generally no more than a liter each, since there are lots of water sources along the trail. The big exception is Death Canyon Shelf. Hikers have to be sure to hydrate before setting out on the shelf and carry adequate water for the journey. There is virtually no shelter or shade along the way so it can be a hot, dry few miles. We carried a water filter to eliminate the "baddies" from our water before we drank it. I still have and occasionally still use that filter. Nowadays though my preferred method for sterilizing water is a SteriPEN which uses ultraviolet light to kill the "baddies." It is lighter and smaller than a filter but is dependent upon fresh batteries to work.

The next day our goal was the South Fork of Cascade Canyon where we had a camping permit for the night. To get there we had to gain quite a bit of elevation to reach Hurricane Pass. This segment of the journey was probably the most scenic though every day offered striking vistas. We hiked though meadows choked with wildflowers, across beautiful streams and through the exposed Hurricane Pass. Hurricane Pass offers one of the very best vantages of the Grand, Middle and South Tetons – a view that the casual visitor to the park will never see since it is from the "back" side of the continental divide – opposite of the park entrance, away from roads and most of the trailheads. From the pass we descended a series of steep switchbacks to reach School Room Glacier where we snapped a few photos and then headed down the canyon to find a campsite below treeline.

I was very concerned about bears here in this beautifully forested and somewhat remote part of the park so I was very careful to hang our food bag a good distance from our tent – and well out of the reach of hungry and/or curious bears. Soon after we set up camp a big thunderstorm roared through. The rain was torrential and the thunder and lightning dramatic. Another group of hikers appeared at the height of the storm and horned in on our campsite. They were drenched and looked quite exhausted. Still, camping "on top" of another party in sites designated for individual parties (as opposed to "group sites") is a pretty big breach of park protocol. On top of their indiscretion they were noisy. After the storm passed and the skies cleared I spoke briefly with them and they were unwilling to move on. The last thing anyone wants is a conflict in the backcountry so I didn't make an issue of it. Other than our noisy neighbors, the night was uneventful. I let Austin sleep in for a while the next morning while I explored the woods around our campsite and prepared breakfast. As I was boiling water for coffee, two deer wandered right into our campsite. I stood very still and they walked within a few feet of me. Clearly they did not see humans as a threat. We ate, broke camp and prepared to set out on the last leg of the journey. Our neighbors still had not ventured out of their tent.

We had not been on the trail long when another deer wandered out of the woods and walked right up to us. Austin had missed the earlier deer encounter so I was happy that he had a chance for a bit of interaction with the local fauna. A bit further down the trail we spotted a moose with a fairly large rack about 50 yards off the trail in a swampy area. It didn't seem too interested in us. As it continued to graze we continued down the trail. This day was all downhill – all the way to Jenny Lake, where we took the boat across the lake to the trailhead and parking lot. We had made arrangements for someone to drive our car from the tram in Teton Village to the parking lot at Jenny Lake. It had been a terrific four day/three night backpacking excursion covering a bit over 30 miles.

Two days later – after a rest day at the Climber's Ranch – we met Calvin Hebert at Exum's headquarters in the morning. This was the beginning of our trip up The Grand Teton. After a quick equipment check we set out for the Lupine Meadows Trailhead and Garnet Canyon. I found the hike up Garnet Canyon to The Lower Saddle – the saddle between The Grand Teton and The Middle Teton – to be quite strenuous, particularly the last thousand feet or so which are pretty steep. The trail covers about 5 miles and nearly 5,000 feet of elevation gain. It offers terrific views of the Middle Teton and other nearby peaks and glaciers but there are very few glimpses of the Grand until one reaches The Lower Saddle. It seemed that every time I took my training to another level and improved my fitness and stamina I found that the mountains to which I aspired required even more. As we got within a few hundred feet of the Exum camp the skies darkened and we experienced a brief summer snow and hail storm. It was short lived and before long we reached the saddle.

Exum maintains a permanent camp at The Lower Saddle during the summer with a hut and a few tents. Their competition, Jackson Hole Mountain Guides, maintains a camp a bit lower on the mountain and off to one side of the approach trail. Most of Exum's clients are packed into their hut overnight in very tight quarters. Since Austin and I were "private clients" and not part of a group we had a tent to ourselves, complete with cushy sleeping pads and lovely down sleeping bags – all provided by Exum. Clients bring their own food on Exum's Grand Teton climb but Exum provides boiling water for completing freeze-dried meals, instant rice and potatoes and such. After a meal and bit of star-gazing it was time to turn in. We were to awaken at 3:00 AM to proceed further up the mountain.

It got pretty cold that night. My little pack thermometer said 22 degrees when I crawled out of the tent the next morning. It was dark, cold and breezy as we choked down a cereal bar and a welcome cup of instant coffee – hot chocolate for Austin. We had brought along very lightweight gloves but our hands were still cold. We could not wait for the sun to rise to take advantage of some solar heat. We set out up the much steeper but still non-technical approach to the Upper Exum route in the dark. As we surmounted a few steep sections that required the use of hands for balance we realized that many of the rocks were covered in ice, remnants of the snow that had fallen the day before and refrozen overnight as ice. As we turned a corner and mounted Wall Street – a wide ledge/ramp that traverses along the southwest face of the Grand - the sun began to rise. Austin complained that he did not feel well. He had the symptoms of AMS – headache and nausea. I gave him ibuprofen and we pushed on to the end of Wall Street. The guides call this the point of no return. This is where climbers rope up and step across a gaping drop-off that could result in a fall of close to 1,000 feet if one were to blow the move un-roped. It is appropriately called "the step-across." It is considered the point of no return because it is difficult to reverse the move and return to Wall Street from the other side. Some consider it safer and easier to climb all the way to summit and take the standard decent than to try to reverse that move. The other side of the "step-across" is where the Upper Exum route officially begins.

    We had a decision to make. Would we gamble on Austin's AMS or turn around and ensure relief at a lower elevation? We had invested quite a bit in this expedition – time, training and money – but clearly health and well-being came first. He wasn't feeling any better so we elected to return to the Lower Saddle. By the time we reached Exum's camp Austin felt fine. Dropping down a thousand feet – sometimes less – usually does the trick, but we had missed our shot at the Grand – one of the most iconic mountains in the United States. Once again, I vowed to return. I was starting to accept what I had read in numerous books - that mountaineering, and achieving summits safely entails a fairly high failure to success ratio. Maybe I needed a new definition of success.

Austin on the Grand Teton near where we turned back

We rested at the Lower Saddle for a few hours then hiked all the way back to the trailhead. I made arrangements for Calvin to meet us a few days later at a place called the Petzoldt Caves, about 1,000 feet below The Lower Saddle on the approach to the Grand Teton. Our plan was to climb a seven pitch rock climb called Irene's Arête. Later that day I spoke with my friend and sometimes climbing partner, Billy Salter, who decided to fly to Jackson and climb with us. He made arrangements for a second guide since Exum had a two client per guide maximum on technical rock climbs. None of us were experienced or accomplished enough at the time to take on this particular route without a guide. We decided to do a guided ascent of Irene's Arête then tackle the Middle Teton unguided the next day. The standard route up the Middle Teton is steep and can have snow-covered sections but is generally considered non-technical.

I secured camping permits for us – one night at the Petzoldt Caves and two nights just a little lower on the mountain at a place called The Meadow. We picked Billy up at the airport a few days later and hiked up to Petzoldt Caves which is just above Spalding Falls. The falls can be quite impressive when there is sufficient snowmelt to sustain it and that section of the trail, just to the climber's right of the falls, is one of the steepest sections. It switchbacks many times and is longer than it looks from the bottom of the falls. We arrived at the caves in plenty of time to set up camp and prepare a leisurely dinner while enjoying the sights. There is a pretty steady stream of climbers and hikers going up and down the Garnet Canyon Trail. It provides access to numerous rock climbs and the summits of the Grand, Middle and South Tetons as well as Cloudveil Dome and Nez Perce.

The next morning we were up early. Our guides were to meet us at 8:00. They started out at the trailhead around 6:00. It takes me (and most mortals) a bit longer to gain the 3,000+ feet to our rendezvous but mountain guides are almost unbelievably fit, second only to porters in my opinion. We snacked on cereal bars and broke camp, stowing our camping gear in one of the nearby caves. Calvin and Bill (Billy's guide) arrived just a few minutes after 8:00. They took a well-deserved rest while we all got acquainted then we took the short off-trail traverse to the start of our route. Irene's Arête is the sharp vertical edge of a prominent outcropping that juts out from Disappointment Peak and which towers over Garnet Canyon. An arête is simply an outward facing corner. It is the opposite of a dihedral which is an inward facing corner. The arête is perhaps 1,000 feet tall and is visible from many vantage points along the Garnet Canyon Trail. From some perspectives it looks like the pointy end of a slice of cake. As far as difficulty goes, most climbers consider Irene's Arête to be moderately difficult. Climbing and mountaineering routes are rated for difficulty and commitment on three somewhat arcane scales. There is (at least) one other scale to rate the difficulty of ice climbs and yet another to rate the difficulty of aid climbs.

    Let's back up for a minute. While there are many different types and styles of climbing they all fall into one of two broad categories: free climbing and aid climbing. Free climbers attempt to ascend their chosen route without the aid of gear which may be attached to the climbing surface – either temporarily or permanently. That is not to say that they do not attach gear to the surface - most do. They just do not use it to aid their ascent. Their rope and gear placements are only to prevent disaster in the event of a fall. Conversely aid climbers place gear with the intention of actively using it to climb their chosen route. Your next question is likely to be "what about people who climb with no gear (and no rope) at all?" That is called free soloing. Free soloists are among the most daring of athletes as the smallest mistake (or event beyond the climber's control) can have dire consequences.

Let's take one step further into the lingo of rock climbing and mountaineering – difficulty ratings in particular. Most serious mountaineering objectives carry a general difficulty rating – called a grade. It has nothing to do with the technical difficulty of any one section of the route but is intended to be a guide to the overall challenge and commitment associated with the route. The scale covers Roman Numerals I through V. Simply stated Grade I routes can generally be accomplished in less than a full day and require little expertise or experience. At the other end of the scale Grade V routes take multiple days, require significant knowledge and experience, entail significant commitment and carry serious risks.

The next scale deals with the difficulty of the terrain. It is called the class. The scale goes from 1 to 5. Class 1 is hiking in the mountains – on or off trail. Class 2 covers steeper terrain where scrambling and occasional use of hands may be required. An ice axe may come into play. Class 3 is generally even steeper and often requires use of the hands. The consequences of a fall may be severe. Some parties may choose to use a rope and gear for protection. Class 4 involves exposed climbing in steep, but not technically difficult, terrain. Many parties will chose to rope up here. A fall could result in serious injury or death. Class 5 is similar to Class 4 but technical rock climbing skills are required. Most parties will use a rope and gear on Class 5 terrain.

All class 5 routes are further rated for just how much technical climbing skill (and strength) is required – i.e. how difficult is the actual climbing. This scale appears after a decimal which separates it from the Class rating and goes from 1 to 15. The decimal in this rating system does not operate like the decimal in the mathematical decimal system. It is merely a separator. To further muddy the waters routes rated 5.10 and higher are often further rated on an a through d scale. Ratings like 5.10b and 5.11c are not uncommon. As a frame of reference 5.1 through about 5.6 is considered fairly easy. 5.7 through about 5.9 or 5.10 is considered moderate and routes with higher grades are considered quite challenging. While the exposure may be disconcerting, reasonably athletic individuals can generally climb 5.5 or so on their first attempt. As you might expect, difficulty ratings are highly subjective. Ratings are usually provided by the first ascent party and may evolve based on consensus of climbers over the course of many years. There is often (but not always) a degree of rating consistency within specific climbing areas but difficulty ratings can vary widely from one climbing area to another. Some climbing areas are well known for "sandbagged" ratings – ratings that underestimate the difficulty of the routes. Here's my personal interpretation of the rating system – at least in an ideal world:

5.0	Rarely used.
5.1 – 5.3	Easy. Not much harder than climbing a (steep/long) ladder.
5.5 – 5.6	Still fairly easy but steeper and/or fewer/smaller hand and foot holds. In some notoriously sandbagged areas (sometimes referred to as "old school" ratings) substitute my interpretation for 5.7 – 5.9.
5.7 – 5.9	Harder/Moderate. Strength, endurance, balance and precision start to come into play.
5.10 a-d	Difficult. Steeper with fewer and smaller hand and foot holds. Climbing technique and strength to weight ratio both become important.
5.11 a-d	Very difficult. Advanced skills and strength to weight ratio are

	required.
5.12 a-d	This is the realm of seriously advanced climbers. Such people are typically dedicated athletes. They are typically tall, strong and lean with excellent technique.
5.13 a-d	A small percentage of climbers can climb at this level. Climbing at this level requires dedication to training and diet and is unattainable for many.
5.14 a-d	This is the realm of elite climbers. Awesome!
5.15	Only a few dozen people in the world have ever climbed routes at this rating. There are very few climbs with this rating since, in order to be awarded the rating, someone must have climbed it.

Irene's Arête is generally considered to be 5.8 with more difficult variations. It is seven pitches long. This was to be (by far) my biggest and most challenging rock climbing route to date. I was very excited and a bit nervous. I had no concerns about Austin as he was regularly climbing 5.11 in the gym by then. It was a big deal for me when I got up one of the easier 5.10's without falling. Gym climbing (and

Our team on Irene's Arête waiting out the rain

gym ratings) are generally considered easier ("softer") than outdoor climbing. So an outdoor 5.8 could easily translate into an indoor 5.9 - or even harder.

The weather was spectacular as we started out on the first pitch of the route but as we climbed the sky became dark and rain threatened. Calvin led the first pitch and belayed me and Austin as we climbed simultaneously. Bill came next followed by Billy. By the time we reached the first belay station it had begun raining – not hard but steady. We broke out our rain gear from our packs and got as comfortable as we could on the small ledges at the top and bottom of a large flake of rock that formed the belay station. Without the sun it was a bit chilly. From the eastern side of the Continental Divide, particularly when one is close to the towering ridgeline of the divide, it is virtually impossible to see approaching weather systems which inevitably approach from the west – until they are upon you. We waited for perhaps 15 minutes when the guides started talking about retreat. Climbing on wet rock is both unpleasant and dangerous – not to mention the hazards associated with lightning. We had not seen any lightning or heard thunder but we could not see any further to the west than the ridgeline above which was less than a mile west of us. We had obviously invested a lot of time and money in this excursion and I really hoped to avoid a second disappointment in less than a week. Billy had flown all the way from Richmond for a few days in the mountains. The disappointment on his face was visible.

Part of our problem was that retreating became more difficult and more dangerous if we were to bet on the weather and move higher. And nobody wanted to lead wet rock unless there was no other choice. As Bill started to rig a rope to rappel from our perch, I asked our guides to wait ten more minutes to see what the weather did. We could rig the rappel and be ready to go at a moment's notice if the weather further deteriorated. They agreed. Just then we started to see breaks of blue sky in the clouds moving in from the west. Within ten minutes the sky had cleared and a few minutes of sunshine with a pleasant breeze quickly dried the rock face. We were on our way again. The rest of the day was "bluebird." The next pitch is one of the harder pitches on the route. There are several ways to climb it. I followed a crack that is about the width of a fist. I decided to try a technique I hadn't had many chances to use called a fist jam. To execute it one simply inserts a hand into the crack then forms a fist which expands the sides of the hand against the inside of the crack. Done properly it is a very solid connection with the wall and can generally support the climbers full weight. I failed to take into consideration the bit of moisture that remained in the crack from the earlier rain. My fist slipped out of the crack and I fell. Since I was secured by the rope that led up to Calvin I didn't fall far, maybe 5 feet. I was unhurt but it was a bit embarrassing. Once everyone was sure I was OK I immediately became the target of the rest of the team's "gentle" ribbing. Darn – fell on a 5.8!

    The third pitch wanders around the arête to the left. The route then entails a few moves on the face before rounding the arête once again. The left side of the arête was the shady side at this time of day and after being in the sun everything looked just a little different. Austin was climbing just above me. He reached for what he thought was a secure handhold. Once he grabbed it and pulled on it it turned out to be a loose rock sitting on a small ledge. It toppled off the ledge and nailed him right in the face, just below his right eye. It created quite a gash – and for a few minutes quite a stream of blood. As soon as I saw it happen I yelled "rock" so that Bill and Billy would have a chance to protect themselves from the hurtling rock. Fortunately, it deflected off of Austin and away from the rest of us. I climbed up to Austin and used my shirt to clean the wound a bit and determine that it wasn't very deep and that it wasn't life-threatening. We finished the pitch and cleaned it up a bit more at the belay station. We elected to leave it uncovered. Austin was quite brave. He never cried or complained and said that he wanted to push on – not that there was much choice at this point.

The rest of the climb was uneventful but spectacular. We topped out around noon, ate lunch and slogged back down through a very loose, very steep gully. We parted ways with our guides, packed up our gear and headed to The Meadow. Austin's wound healed over the course of the next few days and he never had a scar. That was fortunate for both of us. I'm sure I never would have heard the end of it from his mother if it hadn't worked out so well.

The next day we woke up quite early, well before dawn so that we could summit the Middle Teton and get back down before the frequent afternoon thunderstorms pummel the high peaks. I could not, however, persuade Austin to get out of his sleeping bag. He was understandably exhausted and wanted to take a rest day. I couldn't leave him there so I ate breakfast with Billy and told him to go ahead without me. He climbed the Middle Teton solo that day and came back with some terrific photos. I was more than a little bit jealous but obviously Austin came first. He slept until nearly noon while I sat on a rock and read a book I had brought along. I enjoyed the solitude as I watched the procession moving up the nearby trail to the Lower Saddle. After lunch we explored around the area a bit and waited for Billy's return. The next day we all hiked back to the trailhead. Thus ended that summer's trip to the Rockies. That trip, with its successes and its failures really expanded my alpine experience and buoyed my confidence in the mountains. I felt ready to learn new skills and get a taste of serious mountaineering. Denali was really on my mind.

Chapter 11

Growing Ambitions for Father and Son

Richmond, VA
Fall, 2003 - Spring, 2004

When we returned from Jackson I submitted a photo of Austin, Billy and myself topping out on Irene's Arête to the Richmond Times Dispatch, our local newspaper. The paper had previously published the results of the national championship competition. As a result of the two pieces, Austin became a bit of a mini-celebrity around town. It seemed that everywhere I went people would comment on my son's climbing accomplishments. I was better known as "Austin's dad" in the climbing community than as "Manson Boze." Of course that suited me fine. I was very proud of him. I was also thrilled that he and I had found such an incredible common passion that provided a venue for us to build an awesome bond. I am a very fortunate dad.

In the fall Austin decided to rejoin the Peak Experiences climbing team. He had enjoyed being among the oldest in the 11 and under category the previous year but now he was now in the age 12/13 category and knew the competition would be tougher. After all, he had climbed against the group that had aged up into that category two years before. This would be their second year in the category. This cycle would repeat itself year after year until Austin "aged out" of the youth categories in the year of his 19th birthday – his senior year in high school.

    As fall changed to winter I gave a lot of thought to what I would do the following summer. I knew I wanted to get some experience on a world class mountain and specifically learn glacier travel, crevasse rescue and winter camping skills. I had never set foot on a glacier and had very little experience on snow (other than downhill skiing). Getting to 14,000 feet on Longs Peak was definitely an achievement but doing it in summer – mostly on an established trail - pales in comparison to achieving lesser altitudes in harsh "big mountain" conditions. I researched a variety of mountains, including Hood (Oregon), Rainier (Washington), Aconcagua (Argentina) and even Everest (Asia). I compared a variety of guide services as well. I had met a guide on The Grand Teton named Tyson Bradley who also guided for an outfit in Alaska called Alaska Mountaineering School, which has the somewhat unfortunate acronym "AMS" – the same term for acute mountain sickness. Tyson couldn't say enough good things about AMS and its owners Colby Coombs and his wife Caitlin Palmer. I decided on AMS' six day mountaineering course on Denali in late June. That would give me time to travel to the youth national climbing championship which was always the weekend after Fourth of July weekend after my experience in Alaska. As an aside Tyson and his wife Julie now operate their own guide service in the Wasatch Mountains of Utah called Utah Mountain Adventures.

Climbing on big mountains involves significant expense. First there is travel expense - and getting to Alaska from the east coast is no bargain. Then there are accommodations before and after the actual expedition. It is important to get there in time to allow for late baggage to catch up with you and to allow for travel delays. The same thing applies on the back end as expeditions can easily be prolonged by weather and other factors. The cost of guide services varies widely but is never insignificant. Generally guide fees include food and fuel for the expedition and group gear such as tents, cookware and ropes. Some guide services also rent personal gear like snowshoes, skis, sleeping bags, mountaineering boots and ice axes. Whether you chose to rent or buy personal gear it is a pretty significant investment. Since I did not know if I was going to like the experience and spend any more time in harsh mountaineering environments I elected to rent most of my personal gear from AMS.

There was a fair amount of paperwork to complete to sign up for the course – including a detailed resume of my climbing experience, a fitness assessment and of course a liability waiver. Moving around in the mountains, particularly on glaciers, with heavy packs full of gear requires a fair amount of stamina and most guide services provide a fitness regimen that they recommend to prepare for their various trips. They generally recommend that training start six months or so ahead of the trip. My training that winter and spring included steps and squats as well as hiking in the Virginia hills with a pack full of gallon jugs full of water but mostly entailed running. I figured that if I could run five miles in under an hour I'd be fine. I learned later that my benchmark wasn't nearly high enough for serious mountaineering. Unfortunately there really isn't any practical way to acclimatize for altitude when you live at sea level. Fortunately most guide services include adequate acclimatization time in their trip schedules.

Our course was scheduled to take place on Pika Glacier, one of the smaller glaciers on Denali. It empties into the much larger Kahiltna Glacier, home to Kahiltna Base Camp, starting point for most summit attempts on Denali. The upper reaches of Pika Glacier are just below 6,000 feet above sea level so acclimatization would really not be an issue on this trip. Despite the humble altitude of Pika Glacier (the summit of Denali is above 20,000 feet), due to the extreme northerly position of Denali, harsh snowy conditions exist at much lower altitudes than one might find at lower latitudes. By way of comparison, the Arctic Circle is just north of 66 degrees north. Denali is just north of 63 degrees north, only about 180 miles south of the Arctic Circle. Denver, Colorado is just south of 40 degrees north and Everest is just south of 30

Austin climbs a sport route at Red Rocks Canyon

degrees north. Denali is twice as far from the equator as Everest.

During that winter season I experienced abdominal pain unlike any I had encountered before. After a few days of increasing discomfort I went to my doctor who diagnosed me with diverticulitis – inflammation of one of the diverticula of the colon (the large intestine). Diverticula are little pockets that form in the colon and poke out of the colon. Sometimes food particles get caught in them and, if they don't get flushed out, the pocket can become infected. Left untreated it can be very painful and lead to serious consequences, including death. It is easily treated by antibiotics though and a round of treatment resolved it within a week.

In the spring of 2004, I bought a modest house a few blocks from where Austin went to school. It was further from the gym but Austin could walk to and from school. That would make life simpler for both of us and it was nice to have our own place.

The author after a day of climbing in Red Rocks Canyon

For spring break that year, we decided to go climbing in Red Rocks Canyon, just outside of Las Vegas, Nevada. We flew in to Vegas, rented a car and drove west into the desert. There is a campground with limited facilities there that is operated by the state. It offers individual sites with nice level tent pads, picnic tables and pit toilets but no showers. It is cheap though and very close to Red Rocks Canyon. Red Rocks Canyon is one of the best climbing destinations in the country in my opinion. I say that for a number of reasons. First, it is a lovely spectacular desert setting. It offers climbing for every taste and ability – sport and trad, single and multi-pitch, easy to very hard. Finally, it is only about a half hour drive to the Las Vegas strip. It can be very hot there in the summer and quite cold – sometimes with snow – in the winter months. But spring and fall are perfect with highs in the 80's and lows in the 40's. We thoroughly enjoyed our week there, sampling a variety of climbing styles. Since it was just the two of us we didn't worry too much about what we looked (or smelled) like but every couple of days we visited the nearby climbing gym which offers showers for $5.00.

No doubt the highlight of the trip for Austin was the variety of interesting 30 to 80 foot sport climbs near the entrance to the canyon. For me it was the multi-pitch moderate called Cat in the Hat – a five pitch 5.6 trad route in one of the side canyons well into the main canyon. By our last day there we were pretty beat – and our hands were in rough shape from grappling with the desert sandstone – so we took a day off and toured the Hoover Dam, which is only about an hour from Vegas to the east. It had been another great outing.

Back in Richmond Austin was training for and competing in his first year in the 12/13 age category. Nationals were being held in Sacramento, California that year. Austin did well in the local comps, winning most of them. But frankly, our region was not among the best in the country so it was difficult to know how he would stack up against tougher competition. I had no idea if he would even qualify to go to the national championship but I knew I had to plan as if he were going. I booked my travel to Alaska and from there to Sacramento. Austin was to fly to Sacramento with his mother and sister (my step-daughter) where I would meet them. We planned to rent a car and drive to San Francisco to celebrate Fourth of July and enjoy a "family" vacation. Austin would do a bit of last minute training in one of the climbing gyms in San Francisco before we headed back to Sacramento for the competition. Austin was really too young to spend a week on Denali, even at the humble elevation of Pika Glacier. Besides he had no interest in mountaineering. He was evolving into a talented sport climber. Sport climbers tend to be about the athletic/gymnastic aspects of rock climbing while mountaineers, who reside at the other end of the spectrum, are more about stamina, endurance, exploration, adventure and the tolerance of healthy doses of misery. Our climbing interests were starting to diverge.

 Criteria for invitations to the youth national championship changed again that year. There were to be divisional championships in addition to regional championships. There were already 15 regions. They were allocated so that five divisions were comprised of three regions each. Our division was the entire southeast. The top six climbers from each category at regionals were invited to divisionals so that meant 18 competitors in each category at divisionals. Subsequently the top six climbers in each category at divisionals were invited to the national championship resulting in 30 climbers for each category at nationals. Austin finished second at our regional championship that year. Our memories are little fuzzy about divisionals but I think he finished third, gaining him an invitation to nationals in Sacramento.

Three days before I was to leave for Alaska I came down with a second case of diverticulitis. This time I knew exactly what it was – and I was concerned – not only about the trip but about having a recurrence. I had read that some people are prone to recurrences of the disease and that it could require surgery to correct – a surgery that sometimes resulted in a colostomy. A colostomy is a termination of the colon at a connection in the skin of the abdomen that requires wearing a bag to collect and dispose of feces. The thought was terrifying. I started the antibiotics and left for Alaska. I tried not to think about it.

![Kahiltna Glacier on Denali from the air]

Kahiltna Glacier on Denali from the air

Chapter 12

A Foray into the Big League

Talkeetna, Alaska
June, 2004

*I*t was still daylight when I arrived in Anchorage, Alaska after a long day of flying. I was "flying with the sun" and the days are very long at extreme latitudes in the summertime anyway. I only had one connection – in Chicago and it had gone smoothly but flying "with" the sun is deceiving. Anchorage is over 3,400 miles west of Richmond. The flight from Chicago takes about 6 ½ hours. I had packed in two bags. A large duffel contained most of my gear for the mountain, including my 90 liter (5,500 cubic inch) backpack and a smaller duffel contained my "street" clothes. Between them they weighed nearly 100 pounds. I had grown accustomed to toting (and dragging) big, heavy duffels through airports. My ego didn't allow me to rent the handy luggage carts that airports usually provide. To this day I have yet to rent one – although it is only a matter of time. I've come very close on a couple of recent trips. I was a sweaty mess by the time I reached the taxi stand and headed off for the bed and breakfast I had booked for the night.

The next day I got up early and took a quick walking tour of Anchorage. I was pretty impressed. It was tidy and seemed small for a city of roughly 300,000. That may be because there are very few tall buildings. I had pre-booked a shuttle service for the ride to Talkeetna and my driver picked me up around 1:00 for the 80 mile drive. I was the only passenger. On the way to Talkeetna we passed through Wasilla, hometown of Sarah Palin. Of course I had never heard of her in 2004. Talkeetna is a tiny little town with less than 1,000 permanent residents at the confluence of the Talkeetna and Susitna rivers. It is the staging area for virtually all Denali expeditions so the population swells from April through June, the most popular months on the mountain. Talkeetna has a bit of a Wild West feel to it. There are a few bunk houses/motels, a few restaurants and saloons, a coffee and pastry shop and a few tourist attractions. In addition to climbing, Talkeetna also offers rafting, jet boat and fishing trips on nearby rivers, hunting trips and very popular flights over Denali, some of which actually land tourists on one of the glaciers on the mountain. It is also a stop on the popular Alaska Railroad. There is a large resort just outside of town where many of the tourists stay. It is a bustling place during the summer months.

My driver dropped me off at AMS headquarters which is right on the edge of town and very close to the river. I checked in with AMS and arranged to sleep in one of their tents for the night just a few yards from their building then I went exploring. Denali is about 70 miles from Talkeetna and really can't be seen from anywhere in town because of the tree canopy. I wandered down to the braided river which is wide but shallow and broken into numerous smaller streams in places. The water is cold and moves very fast at this time of year as snow and glaciers at higher elevations experience the spring melt. It is also a milky brown color due to the tons of silt it contains. The river offered a break in the trees and my first glimpse at Denali, clearly visible from over 70 miles away. I even got a somewhat rare glimpse of the summit which is usually shrouded in clouds. It looked pretty big but from 70 miles away it is impossible to get a sense of just how big it is.

My next stop was the town itself. There is a very cool museum dedicated to the history of mountaineering on Denali. It has an impressive scale model of the Denali Mountain massif. It is about 20 feet by 20 feet wide. I had read several climbing guides to Denali and spent nearly an hour comparing the intricacies of the model to the various features – ridges, glaciers and summits - that I had read about. I knew the mountain was big but I was starting to get a better idea of just how big. My next stop was one of the local pubs for a beer then back to AMS to see if any of my fellow adventurers had checked in.

My partners were starting to arrive and the "story" of the week was starting to emerge. Justin, Chad and Thomas, grad school buddies from the east coast, told of meeting a "wanderer" on the way in to town. They were looking for AMS when they came upon a man in his 30's walking up the road. He offered to direct them to AMS but insisted that they let him drive their car, which they had driven all the way from the east coast through Canada to Alaska. The wanderer's name was Humphrey. He told a rambling tale of his exploits which, he said, included a recent stint in prison. After they arrived at AMS, Humphrey wandered off again. Pretty soon another member of our team arrived - Jeff from the Washington, DC suburbs in Northern Virginia. Jeff was to be my tent mate and frequent rope team partner on the mountain. Jeff had just walked over from the nearby gear shop. He told of an encounter with a strange man who had purchased a new ice axe at the shop. The man was regaling the sales associate with bizarre tales of his mountaineering experience and went on to pronounce that ice axes made excellent murder weapons. Needless to say Jeff hoped he never saw that guy again. Before long the sixth member of our crew arrived – Alex from Massachusetts. As we all talked – mostly sizing one another up – it started to become apparent that the guy that Jeff had encountered at the gear shop was indeed Humphrey and that he was indeed the seventh member of our team. To say that we had concerns would have been an understatement.

Our guides who had been busy sorting and packing gear came over to our group and introduced themselves. I was quite surprised to find that all three of them were women – Kirsten, our head guide, Shannan and Amy. Kirsten was a powerfully built woman with a slightly weathered face, common among people who spend a lot of time outdoors. We learned that she also guides heli-skiing and rafting in their respective seasons and, when she's not working, she travels to California, Mexico and beyond to surf – quite the outdoorswoman.

LEFT Our guides/instructors: (left to right) Shannan, Amy and Kirsten

Shannan was tall, blond and very attractive. And Amy was tiny – I'd guess no taller than 5'2" and no heavier than 100 pounds. Her diminutive stature didn't seem to diminish her ability to haul a 50 – 60 pound pack and tow a sled with another 40 – 50 pounds of gear.

    Things didn't really get started until the next morning so most of us walked back into town to eat dinner at one of the local spots. I recall that we went pretty light on the beer consumption as nobody wanted to deal with hangovers on our first big mountain experience. We parted company pretty early and headed back to our respective accommodations. Everyone else was staying in one of the motels or bunkhouses so I went back to my tent alone. The nearly 24 hour sunlight was a bit disconcerting and made it hard for me to get to sleep, along with the constant barrage of thoughts about how the next week was going to go and whether I had everything I needed – and not too many things I didn't.

    The next morning our guides had already begun our orientation and gear check when Humphrey wandered in. He seemed to have very little interest in the proceedings. One of the guides focused exclusively on him while the other two helped us get our packs ready. They offered instruction as we took turns practicing ascending a fixed rope that hung from the AMS shed's rafters. Humphrey was clearly going to be high maintenance. We all did our best to ignore and avoid him as we waited for a call from the airport. While early ascents of Denali involved long, arduous approaches that took weeks themselves, virtually everyone who climbs on the mountain now flies onto it. Bush planes fly out of the Talkeetna Airport and land on various gla-

Our pilot and the bush plane that transported me to Pika Glacier

ciers on the mountain. They have skis attached to the undercarriage of the plane that are specifically designed for this purpose. They are lowered down below the wheels as the plane approaches the snow for a glacier landing. The logistics of ferrying climbers on and off the mountain are substantial and become even more complex when weather disrupts the schedule, as is often the case, sometimes for days at a time. Regardless of which direction one is going, the protocol is to let the flight coordinator know you are ready to go then wait around until they call (or come) for you. Sometimes the wait is mere minutes and sometimes it is days.

    We were called shortly after noon. We scrambled to change from our summer clothes into our mountaineering clothes. Daytime temps in Talkeetna in June approach

80 degrees. Highs on Pika Glacier in June rarely get out of the 40's, though it can feel hotter when skies are clear and the sun hits you both directly and indirectly as it reflects off of the snow. We needed to prepare to go from summer to winter in about an hour. Two pickup trucks took us and all of our gear the short distance to the airport where we helped the guides and pilots load it all on to three bush planes. Before going to the airport our guides had carefully weighed us and all of our stuff. The planes had to be loaded carefully so that we did not exceed the maximum load capacity of any of them. Somehow Humphrey managed to get to the airport still wearing shorts and a T shirt. One of the guides coaxed him into his mountain clothes, which she had to find in his pack. It looked a bit like a mother changing her oversized baby's clothes on a diaper changing table. The plane I was assigned to held only three passengers. The best seat on a small plane is, of course, the co-pilot seat – right, front. I don't remember how we decided – short straw I think – but I ended up in the back seat. On Humphrey's plane there was to be no such simple solution. Humphrey simply announced "shotgun" and asserted his "right" to the best seat. No one argued with him.

As soon as the bush planes clear the runway they start gaining altitude in preparation for landing at 5,000 feet or so after a trip of only about 70 miles. As the perspective changed so did my concept of the mountain. With every mile the mountain seemed to grow exponentially. I had seen a lot of mountains in my lifetime but I simply lacked the words or even the scale to fit this mountain into my mental process. I could feel a knot in my stomach growing tighter. Did I have any business on this incredible mountain? Denali is massive. It is the high point of the Alaska

Range which goes on for many miles in each direction with endless towering, snow covered summits. The complexity – depth, breadth and variety of topographic features - of the Alaska Range as accentuated by an abundance of glaciers, massive rivers of snow and ice driven slowly but relentlessly downhill by gravity in every direction. The steeper sections are dominated by outrageously large spires of exposed rock – granite, ranging in color from light gray to nearly black. The area that contains Pika Glacier is called Little Switzerland, presumably a reference to the resemblance of the jagged peaks to the Swiss Alps.

 As we passed the snow line and began to wind our way through narrow mountain passes the skill of these daring bush pilots became very apparent. At times it seemed as if the tips of our wings might scrape against the granite walls that towered thousands of feet above the snowy glacier on either side of the plane. I held my breath hoping that an errant downdraft didn't alter our course with an inevitable horrific outcome. Before long we had a view of both Kahiltna Glacier and Pike Glacier. We could see Kahiltna Base Camp off in the distance briefly before lining up our landing on the all but deserted Pika Glacier. The features looked just like they had on the scale model I had studied the day before. Pika Glacier is bounded on each side by steep granite walls that tower 1,000 feet or more above the glacier. The walls are scored by gullies filled with snow and ice. Our "runway" had been marked by a series of colorful inexpensive plastic sleds which had been planted vertically in the snow along a stretch of glacier. This stretch had been carefully inspected by earlier parties to make sure there were no dangerous crevasses or bumps which could have disastrous consequences for airplanes and their passengers. As they wait for their plane to arrive, every party that departs the glacier inspects the runway and replaces or replants sleds that have moved or been blown away or buried. The first landing of the season must be a nail biter for the pilot and his passengers!

Our guides got out of the planes first and probed the area for crevasses. Once they were confident the area was safe, we piled out and unloaded our gear. As soon as we were done the three planes took off to continue their mission of ferrying climbers on and off the mountain. I've never been in such a remote place and my mind struggled to take it all in. The solitude was matched only by the breathtaking scenery. Our guides knew we had much to do before we could rest so they were coaching us through loading gear onto our sleds, donning our (very heavy) packs and setting up rope teams. Most everyone who travels on crevassed glaciers does so in a rope team of two or three people. Many crevasses become "snowed over" during the winter months and the snow forms snow bridges that make the crevasses invisible. In late winter and early spring most of the snow bridges are very strong and can generally support quite a bit of weight but as the snow pack melts (and evaporates) in spring and summer the bridges become thin and can fail under the weight of climbers. Some crevasses are hundreds of feet deep. Falling into one could be a very unpleasant experience indeed. Rope teams prevent such tragedies. If one member of the team breaks through and falls in the other member(s) fall into arrest position and keep the fallen partner from falling too far into the crevasse using the rope that connects them. We were to learn much more about this skill and the skill of extracting ourselves and our partners from crevasses as the week progressed.

There are no porters – often referred to as Sherpas[1] in the Himalaya – on Denali. Everyone must carry his or her share of the load – personal gear and a share of the group gear. Porters are common on big mountains in many parts of the world but not in the United States. That's not to say that everyone uses them but most do. Climbers on Denali address the requirement for self-sufficiency two ways. In addition to their substantial backpacks – sometimes upward of 70 pounds – most climbers tow sleds loaded with gear. The sleds are just cheap plastic sleds like you can buy at any department store or hardware store. The air taxi services provide them. Climbers also use a technique called ferrying loads. That simply entails carrying provisions and gear to higher camps in stages. The items are cached – usually buried in the snow and marked with wands – and the party returns to their previous camp for the night. This gradual ascent of the mountain can also help with acclimatization. The expression is "climb high, sleep low."

Our team moved perhaps a mile across the glacier to a spot our guides had selected as our base camp. As we moved about and I became accustomed to my surroundings I noticed additional features that I had not seen at first. There were a few other parties camped on the glacier. One of them turned out to be another AMS group which was guided by Kirsten's significant other. We set up our camp about ½ mile from theirs. I also became aware of the relentless procession of avalanches that crashed down the

---

[1] Sherpa is actually an ethnic designation of a people indigenous to the Himalaya but since they are so well adapted to the rigors of altitude and since many of them make a living carrying loads and setting up fixed lines in the mountains there, the term has become interchangeable (at least in that part of the world) with porter.

granite walls surrounding the glacier. They generally started with a sharp "crack" as the snow/ice broke free at a weakness, followed by a progression of thunder-like sounds as the mass of snow, ice and rock crashed downward. The edges of the glacier were littered with avalanche debris. Clearly these avalanche areas were to be avoided. This was a dramatically beautiful but frighteningly dangerous world. As a member of a rope team a climber is in a solitary world between rest stops. Rope team partners are generally separated by 40 to 60 feet of rope, they are generally exerting and they are also making a certain amount of "personal noise" as their snowshoes or skis crunch across the snow. Even on windless days communication while on the move is difficult. I came to enjoy these periods of isolation.

Pika Glacier surrounded by enormous walls of rock, snow and ice. Notice the avalanche debris field at the base of the gulleys

My tentmate Jeff peaks out from our quarters on Pika Glacier

The latrine

Once we reached the chosen spot there was much to do to set up our camp. Before we could un-rope the area had to be probed for crevasses. We marked off the safe area with green garden stakes (which are called wands on the mountain). This would become an often repeated ritual. Tent sites were next. First we had stomp down the snow to create tent pads so that we would not gradually sink into the snow as it settled under our weight. Once the pads were level and compact we erected our tents, being very careful to make sure that every bit of nylon (tent, fly, tent bag, etc.) were always attached to one of us or to the snow with a few stakes or an ice axe. If a tent or part of a tent were to blow away with a gust of wind on the glacier it might be impossible to retrieve. Then we had to build snow walls around our tents to protect them from wind and potential blizzard conditions. Next we had to dig two giant pits – one for our kitchen and one for our latrine (a bit further from our tents).

Since I am on the subject of latrines I will mention that Leave No Trace ethics are alive and well on Denali. Gone are the days that climbers pooped in a cathole on the glacier or pooped into a common garbage bag which was disposed of periodically in a deep crevasse. Groups on Denali now dig one hole in the glacier into which everyone pees but everyone carries a hard plastic can (called a CMC can – for clean mountain can) about the size of a gallon paint can in which they collect their poop for the entire duration of the trip. They pack it out with them and the cans are recycled. Our group latrine had an odd looking line of 10 gray cans, each with one of our names.

As most of us were busy setting up camp, Humphrey produced a bag of chips from his pack and sat on his butt and watched. He didn't lift a hand to help. Poor Alex had been assigned as his tent mate. The rest of us really felt sorry for him and helped him get his tent set up. It was getting late in the day (though still quite light) as we were putting the finishing touches on our camp. Someone looked up and said "oh shit." We all looked up to see that Humphrey had donned his skis and was heading up the glacier alone. Our guides scrambled into action. Kirsten put on a pair of skis to go after him and sent one of the other guides to her boyfriend's camp. He had a satellite phone and could communicate with the "real world." The third guide stayed with the rest of us as the drama unfolded. Humphrey had about a quarter mile head start by the time Kirsten set out after him. Eventually she caught up with him about a mile or so up the glacier. We obviously could not hear their exchange but they "interacted" for quite some time before they both skied back to camp. Kirsten later informed us that Humphrey had decided to go home. Never mind that the nearest civilization was over 70 miles of treacherous mountain and backcoun-

Humphrey sets out alone

try away, part of it crisscrossed by dangerous rivers and crawling with grizzly bears. She somehow persuaded him to return to camp. We prepared dinner and turned in for the night. Alex was justifiably concerned about sleeping in the tent with Humphrey and Kirsten asked if Jeff and I would mind if he moved in with us for the night. Our two man tent would be quite crowded but of course we agreed.

 We were all awoken about 1:00 in the morning by the unexpected whine of a bush plane circling over our camp. We peeked out of the tent and sure enough a pilot was lining up to land on the nearby "landing strip." It never gets completely dark at night in Alaska in June and July and there was plenty of light for the pilot to land. Before long we heard voices approaching camp and one of them commanded Humphrey out of his tent. Colby Coombs, owner of AMS, a park ranger and an Alaska state trooper had flown onto the glacier in the night to remove Humphrey from the team. Clearly they saw him as just a big a threat to our safety as we did. They packed him up and were gone just as quickly as they had arrived. The rest of the week was rife with Humphrey stories, both true and imagined. My tent mate, Jeff, actually wrote a short article about our experience with Humphrey which appeared in one of the two big climbing magazines (Climbing or Rock and Ice, I forget which).

 The rest of the week was full of lessons and adventures around Pika Glacier. We learned and practiced crevasse self-rescue and partner rescue, avalanche evaluation, cold-weather camping and cooking skills and glacier travel. We did a lot of our moving about in the evening and at night. We found that the snow was more firm when the sun was not shining directly on it which was both safer and

95

The team traverses Pika Glacier

Jeff sets up for self-recue from a crevasse

easier. Before we left AMS headquarters we made a choice between snowshoes and skis to move about on the glacier.

Since I had never really spent any time hiking in them I chose snowshoes, a decision I regretted. I found them "clunky" and awkward compared to skis and they required far more effort. I had also rented plastic double boots from AMS. They were not very comfortable but I eventually mastered the lacing and sock combination to make them bearable. I also found that, after several hours of standing/walking on the snow (particularly standing), my feet eventually started to get cold. They never got numb and I certainly never feared frostbite but I would have been happier if they had been warmer. I now own my own synthetic (composite) double boots – a pair of La Sportiva Spantiks. They are far more comfortable and a bit lighter than any plastic boot I have tried. I bought them for my Aconcagua expedition. They are very expensive but incredibly warm and reasonably easy to walk in.

The highlight of our course was an attempt on a small nearby unnamed "summit." It entailed a trek of several miles across Pika Glacier and one of its tributaries and then a climb up a moderately steep – perhaps 50 degrees – snow slope followed by a bit of rock climbing. Before we got to the steep section we switched from snowshoes and skis to crampons. We then had to negotiate a bergschrund – a crevasse that forms where snow and ice breaks away from a steeper rock wall. It took a few hours for all 9 of us to negotiate the more technical part of the climb and we celebrated together in the dusky light of a very late Alaska night. It was 3:00 AM. After that we had to descend, return to camp, eat, break camp, pack everything up and move

Teammates on the finale of our week on Denali

back to our pickup location next to the airstrip. We had been on the move for over 24 hours and were pretty tired but that is all part of mountaineering. We spent about an hour inspecting the airstrip and "re-planting" a few of the colorful sleds that marked the "runway." Then most of us dozed on our backpacks while we waited for our transportation.

On the way back we flew a different route than on the flight in. We flew the path of the Kahiltna Glacier from its confluence with the Pika Glacier. It was fascinating to see how it changed in color, texture and consistency from its upper reaches to its terminus where it turns in to a braided river. The afternoon was a whirlwind of post expedition logistics – gear check-in, storage and cleaning, evaluations and re-packing. As we de-briefed the guides asked me what I thought I might do next. I really hadn't given it much thought – other than a vague notion of returning for a summit attempt on Denali. They assured me that they were confident that I had the skills and the temperament for it. In fact they even encouraged me to consider a route that is a bit more difficult and technical than the Standard (Washburn) Route up the mountain. They did point out that I needed to be a bit more fit – specifically have more stamina – for a summit attempt. Food for thought – and there would be much thought on this subject in subsequent months and years. I was longing for a hot shower and a real bed so I broke down and rented a room in a Talkeetna bunkhouse. The bathroom was down the hall but it was the lap of luxury compared to Pika Glacier.

   Our group re-convened in one of the local taverns for a group dinner and celebration. Humphrey's name was invoked more than once. The next day I caught a shuttle back to Anchorage. I still had a day or two to kill before my flight to Sacramento so I got a room at a motel and researched nearby hiking opportunities. The next day I rented a car for the day and headed for the nearby Chugach Mountain Range where I did a day hike to a summit that was supposed to have a spectacular view. After a few miles I hiked up into the clouds. Conditions remained socked in all the way to the summit so all I saw from the summit was swirling mist. On the way down I did get a quick break in the cloud cover and was treated to a brief view of Anchorage and the Pacific Ocean in the distance. A bit further along I came upon a female moose walking ahead of me on the trail. I gave her plenty of room and she eventually wandered off the trail and let me pass. The next day it was off to Sacramento.

Austin climbs at the national championship in Sacramento

Chapter 13

Another National Championship

California
July, 2004

*A*ustin and his mom and sister had already arrived in Sacramento and rented a car by the time I got there. We collected all of my gear and headed for San Francisco. We had a few fun days of exploring San Francisco over the Fourth of July holiday with stops at one of the climbing gyms to keep Austin strong and focused. We made plans to watch the Fourth of July Fireworks over San Francisco Bay from a restaurant on the waterfront. It was to be the highlight of the San Francisco excursion. Unfortunately fog rolled in to the Bay Area and the bay remained socked in all evening. We heard the fireworks but couldn't see them. Despite the weather we had a great meal and a fun evening together. The next day we packed up and headed back to Sacramento.

Once in Sacramento I had a couple of meetings to attend, one for the 15 region coordinators where we reviewed things that had gone well and not so well that season and one for people who would be judges at the competition. This was my first year as a judge at the national championship. Many of the region coordinators at the time were also parents. Some of the judges were too. Most of us only judged in the sessions that our children were not competing in. It took time away from Austin but I felt like I was making a contribution the sport we both loved and I enjoyed the level of focus that it required. It also provided perhaps the best vantage point of some of the most talented young rock climbers in the country. I also enjoyed interacting with the "inner circle" of the competition climbing world – the volunteer leadership of USA Climbing, the routesetters and the other judges and region coordinators, a few of whom were accomplished climbers themselves. Some of those young climbers have gone on to be the ones we read about in magazines now, including the top male and female climbers in the US today – Daniel Woods and Sasha DiGiulian.

The first year in each age category is usually a struggle, particularly in the 12/13 and 14/15 age categories where teens are growing and getting stronger rapidly. Things tend to level off somewhat with regard to size and strength by the final two categories – 16/17 and 18/19. Austin finished 9th at nationals that year. The top 4 from each category are invited to join the US Youth National Climbing Team. In the upper three age categories that team travels to the youth world championship. I'll never forget the tears streaming down his face after he fell fairly low on the finals route. He was disappointed (having won his category the year before), but we reminded him that he still had another year in the same category and that he'd be the more senior age. He recovered quickly.

Austin climbing at the New River Gorge

Chapter 14

Growth and Challenge

Virginia and West Virginia
Fall, 2004 – Spring, 2005

By the fall of 2004 Austin and I were making regular trips to the two main climbing destinations in West Virginia – mostly in the spring and fall when the weather is most conducive to rock climbing. The New River Gorge is probably better known as a river rafting destination but it is among the most popular rock climbing areas on the east coast. There are well over 1,000 established climbing routes in the vicinity of Fayetteville, WV – a small town on the New River that is the unofficial center of climbing activity there. There is a roughly even mix of trad and sport routes, nearly all of which are only one pitch, and range from 25 feet or less to over 100 feet. There are numerous campgrounds in the area but the one most popular among climbers is called Roger's Rocky Top Retreat. Sadly Roger closed his campground recently and has moved on to other pursuits. For years though he provided a friendly greeting and a slightly unlevel spot for climbers to pitch their tents. It always amazed me how well he remembered people, even infrequent visitors.

The other world class climbing spot in West Virginia is called Seneca Rocks. Seneca is nestled in the West Virginia mountains more than an hour's drive from any significant population center. It is about an hour west of Harrisonburg, Virginia. While the New River Gorge and vicinity is probably best known as a sport climbing area, Seneca is all trad. Most of the routes are two to three pitches. There is more of a feeling of adventure climbing and exposure at Seneca than at "The New," at least in my opinion. As you might have guessed, I favor Seneca and Austin favors "The New."

Both places hold fond memories for us. I executed my first lead at Nelson Rocks, just a few miles from Seneca, while climbing with Bill. It was just a 25 foot sport route with a low difficulty rating but it was plenty scary for me. Back at Seneca on another trip with Austin I was cooking dinner at our campsite after a day of climbing when Austin announced that he was going to go for a run. He was just a little boy, maybe nine or ten years old. He'd never been for "a run" before but had seen me head out to run for years. After only a minute or two I heard a blood curdling scream from a few hundred yards down the gravel road. I took off running to find that he had tripped on a rock or root and done a face plant into the gravel. He had a nasty gash in his forehead near his eyebrow and blood was streaming down his face. We were quickly off to the closest hospital in the small town of Petersburg, WV for a few stitches. Austin was incredibly brave. There were no tears. The nice young intern that sewed him up seemed quite impressed. We actually climbed the next day.

Most of my memories of the New River Gorge revolve around camaraderie with fellow climbers and Austin, sometimes at the odd collection of nearby restaurants and sometimes around campfires at one of the campgrounds. Climbing and climbing destinations are all filled with "characters." The sport seems to attract non-mainstream people, independent thinkers and individualists. While it is impossible to lump all climbers into any one category, most of us do like pitting our skills, experience, training and savvy against challenging physical and mental problems that have consequences for failure. While not a climber, one of the characters we came to know is Brian, the proprietor of the Chestnut Creek Campground at the New River Gorge. In my opinion Chestnut Creek is the nicest campground there – separated, wooded sites with flat tent sites and fire rings, no trash, clean and functional showers and restrooms and a reasonably well enforced quiet time after a certain hour. In the rough and tumble world of campgrounds such order does not come without a price. To say that Brian is meticulous would be an understatement. He has pages of rules posted throughout the campground and he patrols the grounds regularly on his golf cart. He keeps notes about his customers on a tattered yellow legal pad and he can tell you of infractions to the rules you may have committed years before. He's a friendly guy though and, if you don't intend to party until the wee hours, it's hard to find a better place to camp at the NRG.

That fall I had yet another round of diverticulitis. This time my doctor recommended that I get the surgery as soon as I recovered. The surgery entails removal of about the last foot of the colon and, if all goes well, re-attachment of the remaining two feet of colon to the rectum. If things don't go so well the patient ends up with a colostomy, either temporarily or permanently. I scheduled the surgery for the day before Thanksgiving. There was to be no turkey for me that year. Fortunately for me the surgery was a complete success and I left the hospital three days later with my plumbing intact. It took several months to recover from the surgery though. It was a week or so before I could walk more than a block, about six weeks before I could run and months before I could climb. I did not regain my prior level of fitness until nearly summer. I was told that recurrence of diverticulitis is almost unheard of once a patient has had the surgery.

Austin hamming it up with his 4th place plaque at nationals in Boston

In the spring, Austin's second year in the age 12/13 category Austin climbed well. He won our regional championship and finished third at our divisional championship. He went on to finish 4th at the national championship in Boston and, for the second time, got an honorary invitation to join the Youth National Climbing Team. Austin had lofty ambitions for his climbing career but that was to be his last top ten finish. Each year the sport seemed to attract better and better athletes and the more serious climbers definitely trained harder and with more focus. In short the competition got noticeably stiffer every year.

Austin near the summit of Mt. Washington, NH

Chapter 15

New England Adventure

Rumney and North Conway, New Hampshire
July, 2005

After nationals Austin and I drove up to New Hampshire for a week or so of climbing and hiking. We climbed for several days at Rumney, one of the premier sport climbing crags in the country, then headed up to North Conway to explore Crawford's Notch, Mt. Washington and Whitehorse and Cathedral Ledge. We ascended Mt. Washington via Huntington Ravine - a very "sporty" day hike. It is a spectacular hike but I don't recommend it unless you are in pretty darn good shape. I was exhausted and sore to the point of cramping by the time we got back to the car that evening. The summit of Mt. Washington is supposed to be the windiest place on earth. The highest wind speed ever recorded on earth occurred there – in excess of 200 MPH. True to form stepping onto the summit ridge as we ascended was like stepping into jet blast. The winds that day were a "tame" 40 MPH with gusts to 50. We had hoped to climb at Crawford Notch and either Whitehorse or Cathedral Ledge but due to a combination of rainy weather and lack of confidence all we did was gawk. In retrospect I wish I had hired a guide to lead us up at least one of the fabled routes there.

On the way home we talked about stopping at The Shawangunks, better known as "The Gunks" in New York State about 70 miles north of New York City. The Gunks are known for heady and challenging trad climbing with sandbagged ratings – similar in some ways to Seneca Rocks, WV. It was raining as we drove south though and we elected to push on. The Gunks is still on my list of "must visit" places. I want to make sure I'm with a "headier" leader than myself though.

Chapter 16

Busy Year

Various Locations
Fall, 2005 – Spring, 2006

Austin was looking forward to his first year in the 14/15 age category, the first category that requires lead climbing at the championship events. Austin had already been lead climbing for years so the transition was nowhere near as difficult for him as it was for some. Still, he ratcheted up his resolve and began to lead with a new boldness I had not seen before. This year we decided to try a different approach to coaching. A man named Claudiu Vidulescu had earned a reputation as one of the best coaches in the country and was coaching kids in the Washington, DC area. His kids climbed at several gyms in the DC area but climbed most at the Earth Treks gym in Timonium, MD. Timonium is about a 2 ½ hour drive from Richmond, assuming no major traffic snafus. Claudiu actually lives in Atlanta where he runs a construction business but (in those days) he commuted to DC several times a month to coach his kids. When he wasn't in town he communicated with his kids by email and gave them all personalized workouts to do in his absence. The logistics and expense of this arrangement were daunting but I agreed to take it on. We would drive to Maryland one weekend every month for two days of training with Claudiu and Austin would work out at our local gym in between trips north. At first that made our relationship with the Peak Team and coaches a little awkward but everyone adjusted and they ended up being very supportive of Austin. In the end though Austin didn't really take to Claudiu's style of coaching and after several months we stopped going to Maryland. Officially I was his coach again – but he was way out of my league. All I could really do was encourage and belay him.

    Claudiu has produced a number of US Team level competitors over the years. He's a likeable guy but, as you might expect of a guy coaching elite athletes, he pushes his kids pretty hard. Austin had become accustomed to a more supportive style of coaching. Truthfully, I'm not sure he wanted to push himself as hard as Claudiu's higher level athletes did. He became somewhat disillusioned with climbing. For the remainder of Austin's climbing career I would watch him vacillate between the level of dedication required of an elite athlete and the more laid back approach of a recreational climber. To this day I think he still struggles with where climbing fits into his life. Claudiu has been the coach of the US Youth National Climbing Team for several years now and continues to coach kids in the Atlanta area. He's also the head routesetter at the biggest climbing gym in the country – Stone Summit – just inside the loop that surrounds Atlanta.

    By 2006, my friend, Bill, had moved to Kentucky. He subsequently moved to Tennessee. He was a college professor and eager to become tenured at a respected university. I still met up with him once or twice a year in West Virginia - sometimes with Austin and sometimes without him - but for a while I did not have a regular adult climbing partner. There was almost always someone to climb with at the gym where I climbed every Sunday and Wednesday for years. At some point I started climbing on a regular basis with Billy, the guy who had flown to Jackson to meet me and Austin in July, 2003 and with whom we had climbed Irene's Arête. Billy is about eleven years younger than me. He was a rising star at one of the biggest local corporations and a remarkably fit athlete. In 2003, he was just starting to climb but he was smart and had been a dedicated athlete for years so his learning curve was short. By 2006, Billy was a solid climber and sound leader. Billy and I decided to go to the Tetons together that summer. We created a tick list of classic routes we wanted to take a shot at, including the Grand Teton via the Upper Exum route, the route that Austin and I had turned back on three years earlier. Billy and I climbed together quite a bit that winter and spring, including several trips to West Virginia.

Climbing partnerships are a little bit like romantic relationships. Sometimes they work out and sometimes they don't. There are always ups and downs. When you spend a lot of time together, particularly in stressful situations you get to see the best and the worst one another have to offer. For the most part, Billy and I got along. We had similar world views and we both put a fair amount of emphasis on safety and active risk management. At first he saw me as a more experienced mentor but, truthfully, it wasn't long before his superior athleticism made him the stronger climber.

2006 was a very busy year. In addition to our various climbing trips and Austin's training, his sister got married that year. There were parties and receptions and her

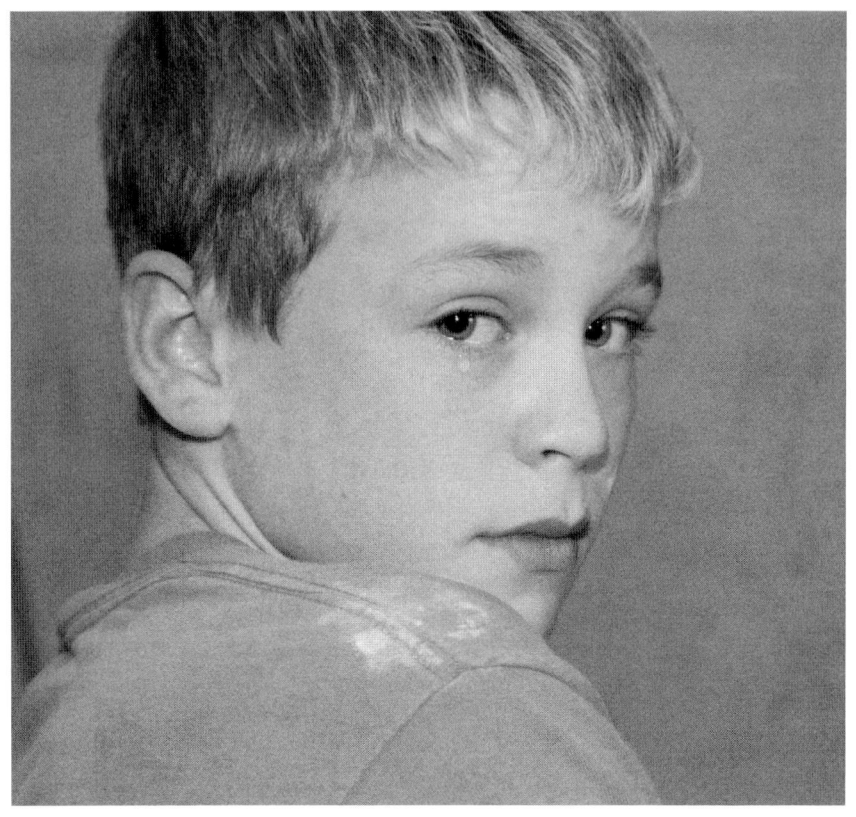

Not satisfied with his performance at a competition

wedding was in Jamaica in June. That spring and summer Austin seemed disillusioned with competitive climbing. He even talked about quitting altogether. He finished 3rd at both regionals and divisionals and 25th at nationals, which was in Portland that summer. I reminded him that 25th in the whole country (within the age category) was nothing to sneeze at.

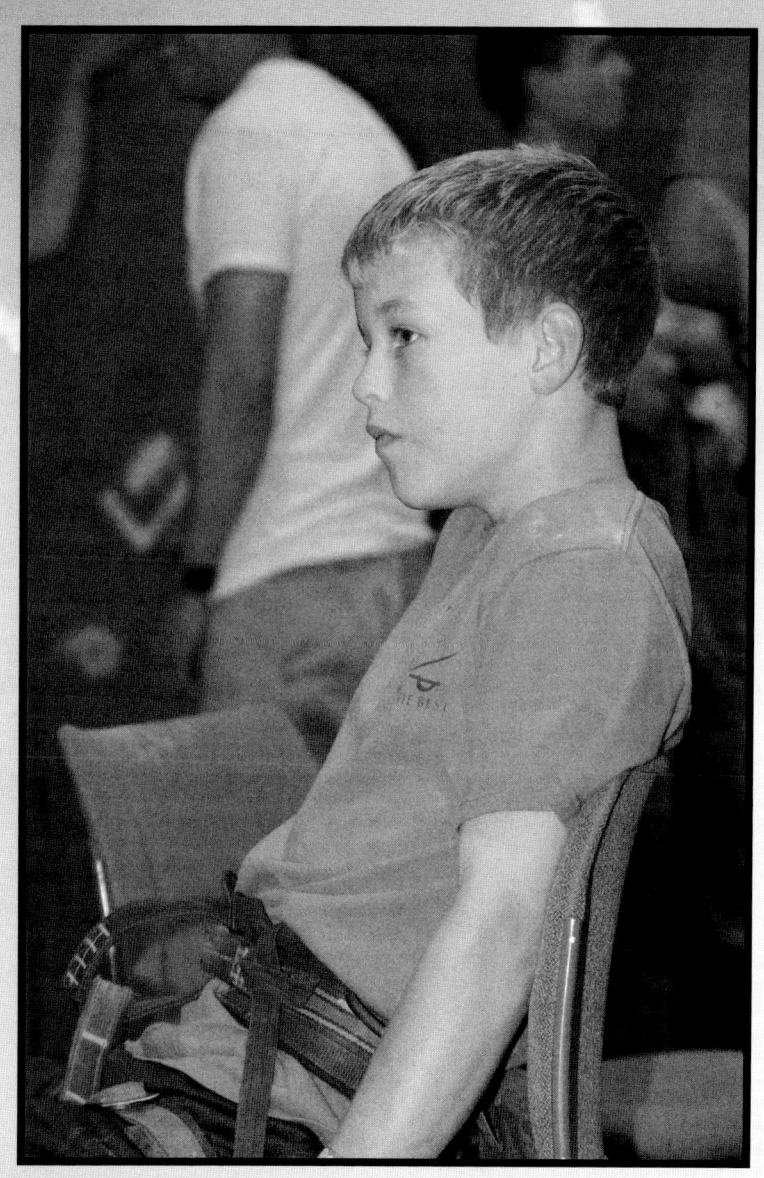

The Tetons are one of the most visually striking mountain ranges in the country

Chapter 17

Back to Wyoming

Jackson, Wyoming
July, 2006

A couple of weeks after nationals Billy and I flew to Jackson. Austin had decided not to go on the summer trip that year, opting instead for basketball camp at the University of Virginia. We had booked a cabin in Grand Teton National Park for the duration of our stay. At about $100/night the cabin was much more expensive than The Climber's Ranch but it had its own shower, there was much more privacy and quiet, and the beds had actual mattresses.

We started out with a warm-up hike off trail in a seldom visited part of the park. We only gained a few thousand feet but it was a great opportunity to stretch our legs and start to acclimatize to the altitude. It was also an opportunity to practice our back country navigation skills (without the aid of a trail and trail markers). It proved to be a worthy adventure on a picture perfect Rocky Mountain summer day. In the steeper sections, Billy's superior athleticism was apparent but, for the most part, I managed to keep up with him.

The next day we were up well before sunrise for a day trip up Teewinot. Teewinot is the imposing sharp summit that stands immediately in front of The Grand Teton when viewed from the east. The east face route we had selected is considered class 4. It is steep right from the trailhead and involves ascending then descending 5,600 feet. The first half or so is established but steep trail. Next there is a snowfield crossing that is a bit scary. The snowfield isn't all that steep (even though it looks very steep from the valley floor), perhaps 30 or 40 degrees but an ice axe is strongly recommended. An unarrested fall would lead to a boulderfield and a steep cliff several hundred feet lower – and certain death.

After the snowfield the climbing gets even more committing for perhaps 1,000 feet or so of steep scrambling up exposed and scree[1] covered ledges. At this point Billy's athleticism really eclipsed my stamina. He was determined to keep up with a party who had passed us and left me in his dust. I continued to climb alone at a slower pace. The skies turned from a luscious blue to a threatening gray. Eventually I met up with Billy who had summited and was heading back down. The summit was only about 300 feet above but the weather looked ominous. Had the skies been clear I would have continued to the summit and returned alone. As it was I chose the safer path and followed Billy down. Downclimbing on class 4 terrain is much scarier (and more dangerous) than climbing up. We had to go slow in order to maintain an acceptable margin of safety. As we climbed down it started to rain, making the rock even more treacherous. Eventually we made it back to the snowfield. It looked even more daunting on the way down – and we

---

[1] Scree is a collection of smaller rocks – pebbles up to softball-sized or a bit bigger.

Just before I slipped on the snowfield on Teewinot

were crossing it in our rubber soled approach shoes. A few feet onto the snowfield my foot slipped out from under me and I started to slide down the snowfield on my back with my feet pointing downhill. We were climbing unroped so I was on my own to self-arrest.

Fortunately my training (from 2004 on Denali) kicked in and I quickly flipped over onto my stomach and assumed the self-arrest position. My ice axe did its job and I stopped only a few feet downhill from where I slipped. It seemed much further to me as I was sliding. I made a mental note that mountaineering boots might be a good investment before my next sojourn across steep snow.

We finished negotiating the snowfield and advanced on to mellower terrain as the rain picked up its intensity.

Billy was more comfortable moving fast downhill than I so he moved on ahead leaving me to enjoy the solitude of the mountain on my own. I was the last man on the mountain that day. It gave me some time to think. I was mildly concerned that Billy had moved on twice that day without me. I wondered what that said about our relationship…and more importantly what it meant for our climbing partnership. It's not that uncommon for partners who travel at different paces to split up in easier terrain so I didn't let myself get too worried. I certainly had not objected to him moving ahead. In fact I'm sure I told him it would be fine.

    Our next objective was Mt. Moran via the CMC route but we had a rest day in between. The approach to Moran involves a canoe so we spent most of our rest day exploring Jackson and renting a canoe, which we strapped to the top of our rental car. The next morning we started out at dawn for the put-in at String Lake. We sealed up our heavy backpacks in extra-large garbage bags in case we tipped over and carefully loaded them into our canoe. Neither of us had paddled in years so it took a few strokes for us to get the rhythm down. We started out with Billy in the stern and me in the bow but it turned out that I was the better paddler – or at least the better steerer. We managed to paddle the length of String Lake, only about a mile, but it wasn't pretty. At the north end of String Lake we had to unload our gear and portage the canoe across a thin spit of land, perhaps a quarter mile, to Leigh Lake, a much bigger lake.

    At Leigh Lake we switched positions and performed far better. Good thing. The Leigh Lake crossing entails perhaps two miles of paddling across a wide open expanse of water. It was pretty calm that morning but with any wind at all it could be a difficult crossing. It took us about an hour or so to paddle across the lake where we finally reached the trailhead for the CMC route. It is possible to hike to the trailhead but much of the hike is off trail and, we were told, entailed some difficult bushwhacking. We stored the canoe at the base of the fairly steep trail. There

Billy on the steep approach - Mt. Moran

were already two other canoes there. The trail is really more of a steep rock-hopping ascent of a rocky stream bed. Our packs each weighed nearly

60 pounds so it was not a casual jaunt. We had climbing and camping gear and food for three days. We expected to complete the approach to the spectacular CMC camp at 10,000 feet on day one, tackle the technical section to the summit and return to camp on day two, then exit the mountain and paddle out on day three. The weather could

not have been more perfect. It was a bluebird day with temps in the 70's.

    After about 4 hours and roughly 3,000 feet of elevation gain we arrived at CMC Camp where we found a number of tents pitched. We learned that the guide services each leave a few tents pitched there all summer for their clients to cut down on the weight they must haul in and out each time they are hired to guide the mountain. As we arrived at camp we encountered another party on their way out. The party was comprised of a guide and three clients. It was fairly late in the day, maybe 4:00 or so and they had just returned from the summit. They reported that they had started out before dawn that morning. They looked pretty beat but they were all fairly young and fit. Wow, perhaps this was a bigger undertaking that I had anticipated. I was certainly feeling the impact of hauling my load up a steep 3,000 foot approach – and that wasn't really the hard part. The other group reported that they were the only other people on the mountain and they were going to continue all the way to their boats and paddle out that night. We would have the mountain to ourselves.

    The CMC Campsite sits on a tree-lined ridge just below the tree line on the south face of Mt. Moran. It offers spectacular views of Jackson Hole and the Teton Range. It is probably the most picturesque place I have ever camped. It is worth noting that the term Jackson Hole, though it is often used to refer to the city of Jackson, Wyoming, actually refers to the picturesque valley to the east of the Teton Range. Apparently early settlers sometimes referred to valleys as holes. Jackson, as mentioned, is the name of the town. The nearby ski resort also bears the moniker Jackson

Hole and the village at the base of the ski resort is called Teton Village. While I'm on nomenclature, I often hear people refer to "The Grand Tetons." In fact, there is only one Grand Teton. The range is properly referred to as the Teton Range, or just The Tetons. The park, named after its tallest summit, is Grand Teton National Park.

    We set up our tent and went about replacing our water supply from the nearby snowfield and stream. Billy used chemicals to purify his water. I've never been a fan of chemicals and, at the time, was using a reverse osmosis filter. Chemicals are lighter and immune to mechanical failure, a common malady of filters, but some of them impart an unpleasant taste to the water and, frankly, I've never really trusted the ones that claim not to. Naturally my filter malfunctioned and it took me a frustrating hour to get it working properly. I carried a repair kit for my filter but the parts are small and disassembling and reassembling the filter without losing parts can be time consuming and frustrating. Eventually I collected a few liters of water and rejoined Billy at our campsite where we prepared freeze dried meals as the sun set. The temperature dropped rapidly but scene was spectacular as the lights in the valley began to twinkle and the range was silhouetted by the setting sun.

    The alarms on our wrist watches/altimeters went off simultaneously at 3:30 AM. It was dark and cold – mid 30's. We scrambled to munch down a quick breakfast and get moving. I lowered our food bag from the tree where we had hung it to keep it out of reach of marmots and bears. Bears generally do not wander that high on Moran but you never know for sure. I left the bag on the ground and the rope attached to it so Billy could haul it back into the tree after he retrieved his food supply for the day. We tidied up our camp, zipped our tent closed and headed up into the darkness, only able to see the area illuminated by our headlamps directly ahead. We had scoped out the first section of "trail" before sunset the day before. The first section entailed scrambling up some steep but non-technical terrain before eventually merging with a rocky stream bed and adjacent series of switchbacks. After an hour or so we took a break for a snack and watched the sun rise.

    Another hour got us to one of the route's prominent features – Drizzlepuss. Drizzlepuss marks the end of the hiking and the beginning of the technical climbing. It is a free standing behemoth that separates the trail below from the steeper granite face above. The front of it is not steep and it is easily surmounted. To the right there is a steep drop-off of perhaps 100 feet or so to a striking hanging glacier. To the left a steep cliff towers above leading to its own stand-alone summit. The back side is steep and requires a combination of sketchy downclimbing and rappelling. Drizzlepuss is considered the point of no return on the CMC route, mainly because ascending the 1,000 feet of slopey (less than vertical) granite towering above is a big, time-consuming commitment with no easy exits and challenging route-finding, but also because climbing back up Drizzlepuss to exit is considered by some to be the most technically difficult part of the route. Our guidebook offers the following description of the view from the top of Drizzlepuss: "From here there is a terrifying view of the CMC route which goes more or less up the middle of the face to the left of the black dike; most of the slabs appear impossible. However, take heart and downclimb the very steep west face of Drizzlepuss toward the notch separating

Billy examines the steep 1,000 foot headwall at the top of Moran from the top of Drizzlepuss

it from the main east face of Mount Moran."

My altimeter read 11,730 feet. The summit of Moran is at 12,605 feet. What happened next I still do not fully understand. It was 7:00 AM. We were right on schedule and it was another bluebird day - but it was apparent that Billy had reservations about continuing on. He correctly pointed out that whatever decision we made, whether to push on or to turn back, needed to be a team decision. He pointed out that we (and by we he clearly meant me) had been moving slow the last few days and that it would be unwise to find ourselves higher on the mountain come afternoon when thunderstorms are the norm in the Tetons, or worse, find ourselves still looking for the way down in the dark. While I don't really know what was in Billy's mind that morning I could not help but interpret his concern as a vote of no confidence in me. I really felt like I had no real alternative to concurring that we should give up our attempt on the summit. I'll admit that the view from Drizzlepuss was both daunting and intimidating but I really felt, and feel to this day, that we were both up to the challenge.

 The decision made to turn back, we were in no hurry to go anywhere. The weather was beautiful and we had 13 hours of sunlight remaining. I belayed Billy down part of the 200 foot downclimb on the back side of Drizzlepuss – a bit of a reconnoitering mission for the future. When he returned he proclaimed it didn't look all that difficult. While Billy was down on the face a particularly aggressive marmot decided that he wanted whatever was in Billy's pack, which he had left on the rock about 15 feet from me. I was anchored and busy belaying so I could not go move the pack and, instead, had to throw stones at the marmot to keep it away from the pack – and Billy's lunch. I felt a lot of emotions on the mountain that morning – and for the remainder of the trip. I was disappointed, frustrated and a little angry. In retrospect I feel like we both failed. We failed to communicate very well. We failed to accept a challenge that we were both fully capable of meeting. And we clearly failed to reach our goal.

 We hiked back down to our campsite where we found the food bag exactly where I had left it – on the ground. Turns out that Billy assumed I was going to go back over there and haul it back into the tree. In the dark that morning we had not seen it laying on the ground as we tidied up our camp. Remarkably the bag and its contents were untouched. We both lay out on rocks and took naps in the sun. As I woke up Billy walked over and pronounced that he wanted to hike out to the trailhead right then and there. I objected. In my mind there was no reason to rush off the mountain. He insisted, saying that he was going even if I didn't. A rather unpleasant discussion ensued. I pointed out that paddling across the lake alone and portaging the canoe alone would be a serious challenge and that he would leave me with no way out. He responded by saying he could handle it and that he would come back and get me the next day. Again, I felt that I had no alternative than to pack up and join him. I was furious but I did my best not to let it show. Once we packed up camp I moved down that mountain as fast as I could within a reasonable margin of safety. Billy may have been holding back to give me some space but I moved away from him fairly quickly and only rarely saw glimpses of him above on the way down.

 Once back to the rocky stream bed about 2,000 feet above the canoe and trailhead I encountered another party ascending the trail, a guide and several clients. The guide, like virtually all guides, looked extremely fit but the clients were not in good shape and were struggling up the "hill." I placed their odds of success at near zero. In fact I wondered if they would even make it to CMC camp.

 Once at the canoes, I prepared my pack for the crossing and dragged the canoe to the edge of the water where I waited for Billy. By now the wind had picked up quite a bit, There were even whitecaps on the lake. Of course the wind was coming directly from the direction we would be traveling in. Our paddle back across Leigh Lake took a grueling couple of hours. String Lake was easier since it is narrow and mostly sheltered by trees. Billy and I barely spoke for the whole trip back to the car. In fact I don't think we even spoke for the rest of the day.

Our plan for the rest of the trip had included a variety of climbs based out of Garnet Canyon including the Grand Teton, but I really wasn't sure what to expect given the meltdown on Mount Moran. The next day we returned our rented canoe and hung around in Jackson. Billy went to visit a buddy of his who was guiding for Jackson Hole Mountain Guides while I wandered around town. We made plans to meet for beers and dinner later at a bar in the middle of Jackson. When we met Billy reported that his buddy was off the next day and planned to climb the Grand in a day – trailhead to trailhead – via the full Exum route – Lower and Upper – a very committing day – and had invited Billy to come along. Of course Billy was all over that. There was never any question of whether I would go. I clearly wasn't invited…and would not have accepted anyway. Such a day was well beyond my capabilities. Even today – and I'd say I'm 40 or 50% more fit now – a day like that is out of reach for me. I agreed to get up at 3:00 AM and take Billy to meet his friend at the trailhead.

While Billy was on the mountain that day I went on a day hike at lower elevations and pondered my next move. I was still angry, frustrated and disappointed. I decided to "get the hell out of Dodge." I wasn't sure if my relationship with Billy could be mended but I was sure that I was done with this particular trip. I changed my airline reservations and booked myself to return the following day. I waited for a several hours for Billy at the trailhead. They were behind schedule. Finally they appeared around sunset – maybe 8:00 PM or so. His guide friend still looked strong but Billy was dragging. He said that it was the most strenuous day he had ever had. I was happy for him that he had summited the Grand and had done so in grand style but it was no comfort to me. I told him I was leaving the next day.

    I left Billy my tent and some climbing gear and we drove to the airport where I turned in the rental car that was in my name and Billy rented another one in his own name. Other than the occasional polite greeting in the gym, we really didn't really speak for months after that. A few years later Billy returned to Jackson Hole with another (uber-athlete) climbing partner and they climbed Mount Moran. To this day I have not been to the summit of Mount Moran or the Grand Teton.

    I've read that mountaineering is as much (or more) about failure as it is about success - better to return safely to try again another day than to make the wrong decision and die or get seriously injured pushing it – but failure was really starting to become the theme of my mountaineering career.

    Eventually Billy and I patched things up and became friendly again. He has moved on in his life in many ways and rarely climbs any more. Oddly enough, after Peak Experiences asked me to teach their lead climbing class in early 2011, Billy expressed an interest in teaching as well. For a while we were the gym's only lead climbing instructors and we each taught one class a month. We don't see each other very often but we get along fine when we do. We are both single now but circulate in different circles. Once in a while we get together for drinks or dinner to commiserate. I bear Billy no hard feelings. I hope he feels the same.

Austin at the New River Gorge

Chapter 18

An Uneventful Year

Virginia, Michigan
Fall, 2006 – Spring, 2007

This year Austin returned to the Peak Team. Bouldering was starting to become very popular and an organization called ABS (American Bouldering Series) organized a competition series that ran through the fall and wrapped up in February. Bouldering is simply climbing on shorter routes called problems – 8 feet to 20 feet tall – without ropes, usually with spotters and always with crash pads. Eventually ABS merged with USA Climbing which ran both the bouldering series and the roped climbing series. At first Austin wasn't really into bouldering but he did compete in some of the local comps. This was Austin's second year in the 14/15 age category. In the spring/roped series he finished first at regionals and second at divisionals.

Nationals was in Ann Arbor Michigan that summer. A fellow named Brent Quesenberry had taken over coaching duties at the gym the year before. The kids really liked him. I did too and we became good friends. I spent quite a bit of time with him in Ann Arbor that July. We travelled to Yosemite together the following summer. As I write this in 2012 Brent is still the head coach of the Peak Climbing

Team and he and I climb and mountain bike together often. Brent went on to become head routesetter at the gym and to become a nationally recognized routesetter. He runs the climbing portion of a popular pro comp held annually in Richmond as part of the Dominion Riverrock extravaganza. Riverrock has running, kayaking, biking, climbing and other competitions along with music and other entertainment. It is quite a festival for both participants (who come from all over the country) and spectators. Austin finished 14th at Ann Arbor. We took a break that summer. There was no big climbing trip but we did go to West Virginia a few times.

Austin climbs in Red Rocks Canyon

Chapter 19

Growth on Several Fronts

Various Locations
Fall, 2007 – Spring, 2008

As we kicked off the 2008 climbing season Austin "aged up" to the 16/17 category. His dedication to climbing waxed and waned but he still spoke of winning another national championship and of making the US Team. Nationals was back in California that year, this time in a gym in San Jose. We made plans to go to Yosemite with Brent after the comp. We also made plans for Austin to attend a climbing camp in California that would be coached in part by one of the world's best climbers – Chris Sharma. He was totally psyched but that meant two round trips to California that summer for Austin, the second one traveling on his own at age 15.

2008 also marked the year of Austin's 16th birthday and the prospect of a driving permit. Knowing that Austin would be driving soon I was ready to move out of the little house near school and find something a little nicer and a little newer. We settled on a brand new townhouse nearby but a bit further from school. He could still walk but it took nearly a half hour each way. We waited until school let out in June before we actually moved. He would not be able to drive to school the following year either but he was certainly old enough and we lived close enough for him to get back and forth with little help from me.

I had started getting more serious about my own training by 2008. A few years before I had set a goal of running five miles in under 50 minutes by my fiftieth birthday. I barely made it – but by now it was fairly routine. I had not run in any sort of race since high school so I decided to sign up for the big local 10k and I set a goal of running it in under an hour. A 10k is 6.2 miles so that meant (averaging) six sub-ten minute miles. The first year I ran the race, 2008, I didn't even come close. I think my time was around 1:08. In 2009 I improved to 1:06. And in 2010 I finally ran it in (barely) under an hour. In 2009 I started running longer distances and more weekly miles. I was feeling confident and signed up for the half-marathon – 13.1 miles – only one week before the race. Mind you the farthest I had ever run at one time was 8 miles. It was a lark but I had nothing to lose. I knew I could walk the rest of the race if I ran out of gas somewhere along the race course. I did manage to finish the race (with almost no walking) but my time was an embarrassing two hours and thirty-five minutes. The following year I improved my time to 2:14 which was better than I expected, though still not even in the top 200 in my age category! I matched that time in 2011. I've probably topped out. I'll never be a competitive runner. I don't have the build (or the dedication). But running is a great way to stay in cardiovascular fitness – as long as the joints hold up. The stamina gained from running makes a huge difference on long days in the mountains.

GROWTH ON SEVERAL FRONTS

In the spring of 2008 Austin and I went back to Red Rocks Canyon. This time we stayed in a beat up old hotel in the desert near the entrance to Red Rocks Canyon. A friend of ours from Richmond who was touring the country in his truck met us there for a week of terrific climbing. Austin was much stronger this time and climbed several very impressive lines – ranging up to 5.12 in difficulty.

Just before we left for nationals that year I experienced a familiar pain in my gut. It was in a new location – they had removed the section of colon that had been problematic before – but the pain was unmistakable. This was not supposed to happen. I didn't let on but, honestly, I was terrified. As before, a round of antibiotics, which I didn't finish until we were in California for nationals, cleared up the immediate problem but I was pretty sure that would not be the end of it. I scheduled an appointment with a colon specialist for August after our return from California to see what was going on and get a recommendation.

Austin won the regional championship that year, finished fourth at divisionals and a disappointing 27th at nationals. He made a mental error on his second qualifying route and failed to make it to the semi-finals. It can be incredibly disappointing to put so much time, effort and emotion into a sport and come up short of your goals. It is easy to lose sight of the fact that you are still in the top 30 climbers in your age category in the entire country. I reminded Austin of that fact often and tried to persuade him that, no matter the outcome, we were still having fun, getting strong, and meeting terrific people.

Austin and Brent climb above me in Yosemite

Chapter 20

Yosemite

Yosemite National Park
July, 2008

We watched the remainder of the competition in San Jose then headed up into the mountains. We had no reservation and planned to camp but getting a site in Yosemite in the summer is a bit of a crap shoot. It is a very popular place. Our plan was to tour Yosemite Valley, the most popular section of the park, upon arrival then drive to Tuolumne Meadows, a less crowded section of the park at a higher altitude with cooler temperatures. "The valley" as climbers refer to Yosemite Valley can be very hot in addition to being very crowded in the summer time. And while the granite walls of the famed domes in Tuolumne are not as tall as the ones in the valley they are majestic and offer endless climbing possibilities. The plan worked. We scored a campsite just as we arrived that evening, perhaps the last one available as we saw lines of people waiting for sites at the gate the entire week we were there starting just after we checked in.

On the way in we drove through a frightening hail storm. The park service actually closed the road for an hour or because of the accumulation of several inches of hail – a reminder that things can change quickly in the mountains and that just beneath the beauty lies danger.

We climbed in Tuolumne for a couple of days but frankly found the climbing pretty intimidating. The routes were fairly run out (long distances between opportunities to place protection) and the slabby walls felt tenuous under our feet and offered few decent hand holds. It was mostly friction climbing. The highlight of the Tuolumne climbing was supposed to be Cathedral Peak, a five pitch 5.6, but weather threatened just as we gained the first belay so we retreated. After the long (about 5 miles) uphill approach we were quite disappointed to turn back without completing the route.

We packed up and headed further east toward Mammoth. Mammoth is a popular ski resort in the winter but the area, the eastern slope of the Sierra Nevada Mountain Range, offers an excellent assortment of climbing opportunities including Austin's favorite, bolted/sport climbing. Unfortunately I did some damage to my shoulder while belaying. It would turn out to be a pesky injury that bothered me for nearly a year until I went to see a doctor and had it surgically repaired. Still, we got in two terrific days of climbing there before heading back to San Francisco to catch our flight. Brent had an earlier flight leaving us with a day to kill so, after we dropped him at the airport, we drove down the Pacific Coast Highway to Monterey where we toured the Monterey Bay Aquarium. Then it was back to San Francisco to catch the red eye back to the east coast.

Two weeks later Austin was back on another flight to San Francisco. At age 15 Austin was an experienced traveler but had never really traveled without one of his parents. Naturally we fretted over every detail of his trip and required him to check in via cell phone after each leg. He even had to catch a hotel shuttle from the airport and spend a night in a hotel alone on each end of his week-long camp experience. The camp picked him up in a van at his hotel and took him back to the mountains, not far from where we had been two weeks earlier but slightly further south – in the vicinity of Bishop, California. The camp was a bouldering camp - no roped climbing. Austin had a blast and was thrilled to be climbing with his hero – Chris Sharma. Chris is one of the few climbers in the world who has climbed routes with the lofty 5.15 rating. The trip went off without incident and he returned safely home.

    I went to see the colon specialist who tried to reassure me but he did seem concerned. After all, recurrences of diverticulitis after a colonectomy are supposed to be rare. He scheduled me for a colonoscopy in September.

Chapter 21

Life Goes On

**Various Locations
Fall, 2008 – Summer, 2009**

When school started in September I was back to driving Austin to school most mornings. It only took a few extra minutes and most days he walked home after school. He was enrolled in driver's education and we were both excited about him getting his license, even though the school did not permit 10th graders to park at the campus. He didn't actually get his permit until spring.

I was worried about what the colonoscopy was going to reveal. Colonoscopies are much dreaded. Physicians recommend that everyone get one around their fiftieth birthday and every ten years thereafter. They sound much worse than they are and, in my opinion, the dread is misplaced. It is a simple but somewhat frightening and, for some, humiliating procedure. A doctor inserts a scope (basically a video camera on a flexible tube) into the anus and snakes the device up into the colon while examining the walls of the colon on a monitor. Fortunately for everyone involved the patient is rendered unconscious with anesthesia for the procedure. There is no sensation or aftereffect. The worst part of the whole thing is the preparation. In order for the doctor to have a clean image of the colon wall the bowels must be empty and clean. That's accomplished by taking a combination of medication and copious amounts of water to purge the system – not painful but not particularly pleasant either. This is done the day/night before the procedure and the patient cannot eat anything until after the procedure. Both times I have experienced them I remember being very hungry.

When I went back to get the report from the doctor I was told that there were a few small diverticula on what remained of my colon but that they did not seem to be anything to worry about. That didn't stop me from worrying. There is no known cause of diverticulitis. Virtually everyone over 50 has diverticula. It is unknown what causes them to become infected in some people but not others. Certain foods are suspected as possible instigators. I was determined to find the cause, at least the cause for me. Over the course of about six months I experimented with eliminating various things from my diet. In January I had another occurrence. I was even more determined to find the cause. I grew to suspect that peanut butter which I ate fairly regularly, often straight from the jar might be the culprit. I stopped eating peanut butter that winter and I have not had a recurrence since. My doctor looks skeptical when I tell him that I am certain that peanut butter is the trigger, at least for me. I don't really care. I am certain that I found the culprit and am happy to be living free from the disease.

Earlier that year my boss at the Chamber had retired and the board had hired another chamber exec from a chamber in Florida to replace him. Over the years I had become very comfortable in my role at the Chamber and had a terrific relationship with my boss and all of my co-workers. I knew that the dynamic would change with new leadership. It was inevitable. In December I elected to leave the Chamber and start my own consulting practice – focusing on human resource management policy and practice and strategic planning for small companies and non-profits. The timing was terrible. As you no doubt remember 2008 was the beginning of a long-lasting economic downturn and my business never really took off. It did, however give me much more flexibility with how I spent my time and, after a couple of years I just decided to retire. My mom had passed away in late 2007, leaving me some financial resources and I had accumulated reasonable retirement assets during my 20 years at a job with a big Fortune 100 company and my 10 years with the Chamber.

This was Austin's second year in the age 16/17 category and the training routine went on as usual. In the fall Austin competed in an outdoor bouldering competition held annually near Boone, North Carolina. This was his fourth appearance at the Houndears competition. Houndears is part of a fall

Austin climbing at Houndears

series known as The Triple Crown. The other two comps in the series are in Tennessee and Alabama. The series is not affiliated with USA Climbing and has its own rules and climbing categories. Each year Austin had gotten stronger and climbed more of the problems. Houndears draws climbers from all over the southeast and a few nationally recognized climbers. The roughly 100 spots available for the competition routinely sell out months before the actual competition. While Houndears offers a youth category (I think it is for climbers 12 and under), it is primarily an adult comp. The average age of the competitors is probably mid-20's but there are usually climbers as young as 10 and as old as 50+. Non-youth climbers are allocated to categories based on their skill level – beginner, intermediate, advanced and open. Except for 2004 when he qualified as a "junior," Austin started out in intermediate and eventually ended up in advanced. He always had fun and enjoyed the problems, but it would not be until 2010, his senior year in high school, that Austin placed in the results.

Nationals was in Salt Lake City that year and we made plans to stay over for a week and climb in the nearby Wasatch Mountains – essentially the western edge of the Rockies. Austin won the Mid-Atlantic regional championship for the third straight year then went on to finish second at the divisional championship. At nationals he came in 18th – ever the bridesmaid and never the bride. I had been suffering from shoulder pain since the previous summer, the result of arthritis and some shredded cartilage. I had elected to have surgery to repair it that spring. I was still healing and had only just been cleared to climb as we left for Salt Lake. My activities that summer were limited mostly to hiking and belaying. I actually climbed very little

Austin climbs at Maple Canyon

for nearly a year in hopes of regaining pain-free use of my right shoulder. We spent time that summer in some fabled climbing areas in Utah including Big and Little Cottonwood Canyons and Maple Canyon. A number of other climbers from nationals stayed over to climb as well so Austin had a blast hanging out with people he generally only saw once a year.

Chapter 22

Steps Along the Way

**Various Locations
Fall 2009 – Spring 2010**

By the time I returned from Utah that summer I had put on a few pounds - and frankly I wasn't exactly svelte before. I was determined to do something about it and enrolled in a ten week weight loss program run by a local weigh loss clinic. The program started in late August. By the time it wrapped up in November I had lost nearly 20 pounds. More importantly I had a much better understanding of how the body reacts to various foods and eating habits and I had refined my workout routine. My diet and exercise routine is still largely influenced by what I learned. I started climbing again that winter and, once I regained some of my climbing stamina, I was quickly climbing at a higher level than ever before – at the not-so-youthful age of 54.

As mentioned earlier it was November of 2009 that I ran my first half-marathon. While my time was nothing to brag about the effort was inspired in part by success in the weight loss program and I was very happy indeed just to finish the thing – and with almost no walking! I began to think that loftier alpine goals might be attainable. I even started to think again about returning to Denali.

It was Austin's junior year in high school. Between training, schoolwork, researching potential colleges and taking the College Board tests, he was pretty busy. He had begun to express a strong interest in the University of Colorado at Boulder so we used his spring break that year to travel to Boulder, visit with the admissions folks and take a tour of the school. We had passed through Boulder several times on our various trips out west and Austin had older friends who had chosen schools in Colorado including CU. While we were there we climbed in one of the renowned climbing gyms that Boulder is known for (among climbers) and visited two others. Austin fell in love with the place. This was clearly his first choice.

In the spring Austin got his driving permit and I bought "us" a second car – a Nissan Xterra. My primary car was a coupe and wasn't much good for climbing trips plus it had a manual transmission and Austin never really mastered driving it. The Xterra would be great for climbing trips and anything else that required a larger vehicle. As you might have guessed it pretty quickly became "his" car.

Rumors had been circulating for quite some time of a new gym to be built in Atlanta. It was to be the biggest climbing gym in the country. In the summer of 2009 it was confirmed that the gym was under construction and everyone expected it to be completed in time to host the youth national championship in 2010. Climbers all over the country eagerly monitored the internet for progress reports and photos. Meanwhile Austin landed a second place finish at regionals and a fifth place finish at divisionals, his first year in the age 18/19 category. This was to be Austin's 8th consecutive appearance at the youth national sport climbing championship. Neither of us took that for granted but it had become part of our summer routine and we looked forward to seeing the new gym in Atlanta. We also made plans to drive directly from Atlanta to Boulder, Colorado after the comp for two weeks of climbing. We were very excited. I was particularly looking forward to it as I sensed that it might be my last summer trip with Austin. He would graduate from high school the following summer and head off to college.

The new gym, Stone Summit, was everything we anticipated and more. In my estimation it is nearly twice as big as the largest gym we had ever

The climbing wall at Stone Summit

been in before and beautifully appointed. The competition was spectacular, definitely the best one we had ever seen. Austin finished 23rd. Frankly I feel he was negatively impacted by what I considered to be less than ideal route setting choices by comp officials. I rarely complain about actions and decisions by comp organizers. I know how difficult it is to execute a competition of this magnitude (over 400 competitors) and how complex it is to set appropriate routes for five different age categories in both genders that test a variety of climbing skills while offering enough, but not too much, of a challenge. That said, both of the qualifying routes for the male 18/19 climbers that year were "roof marathons." That is to say that the majority of each route was set in extremely steep (as in climbing on a ceiling) terrain. Steep terrain goes with the territory in the older categories but for both routes to test the same skill set seemed in my mind to favor athletes for whom that style was a forte. At the end of the day though my opinion really doesn't count and we both had to get over it. Route style from the perspective of the climber is just the luck of the draw.

After the comp was over – nationals is a three day affair – we hopped in the car and drove straight through to Boulder, with stops only for gas and food…and one two hour nap in a rest area.

RIGHT Looking down from a belay stance on the First Flatiron. Austin, Boulder and the University of Colorado below.

Chapter 23

Another Trip to Colorado

Boulder & Estes Park, Colorado
July, 2010

Seventeen hours after leaving Atlanta we were in Boulder. We planned to spend the first week climbing in and around Boulder so we checked in to the Boulder International Hostel. The hostel is right next to the campus of the University of Colorado at Boulder. By now Austin was pretty sure that CU was where he wanted to go to school. The Boulder International Hostel is far from luxury accommodations but it is one of the best deals in Boulder. We climbed for several days in Boulder Canyon and the Flatirons as well as Movement Climbing and Fitness, one of the newer (and nicest) climbing gyms in the country. Boulder Canyon offers a variety of climbing styles but includes a lot of sport routes, Austin's favorite. The Flatirons entail mostly trad climbing, my favorite. He indulged me by leading some of the scary pitches up the first flatiron. That was really his first trad lead. He actually seemed to be enjoying it. Of all the routes we did that week though I think his favorites were in the gym. We had driven 1,700 miles to climb in a gym! Oh well. We were having fun.

Austin is taller than me . . . but I'm finally in shape!

It was very hot on the Front Range that summer so we decided to head up into the mountains in hopes of cooler temps. We drove to Estes Park and checked in to the Colorado Mountain School Lodge.

The lodge is another bargain for climbers. It is basically a bunkhouse with showers, rest rooms and a shared kitchen. But it is clean and it's staffed by CMC climbing guides who are happy to make suggestions and share beta.

We climbed one day on The Book, one of the prominent features of Lumpy Ridge. Austin led several pitches. I was very pleased with most of his gear placements. We had talked about attempting the Ypsilon traverse the following day but, after consultation with the CMS guides settled on a less committing endeavor. The guides were in concurrence that the Ypsilon traverse was a very challenging outing even for them and that it often took uber-fit types 14 to 16 hours to complete. The climb entails about a 5 mile or so approach with maybe 4,000 feet of elevation gain followed by another thousand feet of climbing and scrambling along a dramatic ridgeline, the Blitzen Ridge, to the summit of Ypsilon Mountain. The descent follows an opposing ridgeline called the Donner Ridge. The two ridges form the enormous granite cirque that surrounds the Spectacle Lakes. I have admired these two ridges and the scene across the lakes from the rocky shoreline of East Spectacle Lake on two occasions now and, each time, longed for a tour of the ridge lines that tower 1,000 feet above. Maybe one day.

Meanwhile, at the guides' suggestion we settled on Notchtop via the Spiral Route. Notchtop is a spire that is partially detached from the main rocky ridgeline of the continental divide as it cuts through Rocky Mountain National Park. It also entails about a 5 mile approach but with perhaps only 3,000 feet of elevation gain, followed by a bit of off-trail hiking and several hundred feet of scrambling up a steep and somewhat loose gulley to reach the beginning of the technical climbing. Once the summit is attained it is possible to rappel back to the point where the technical climbing began. The route

Notchtop bathed in alpenglow

derives its name from the fact that it winds 360 degrees around the spire on the way up in the shape of a spiral. At 5.4 the climbing is fairly easy but routefinding provides an interesting challenge, both on the way up and the way down. We didn't even carry technical climbing shoes, electing instead to climb the whole thing in our approach shoes.

We were up at 3:00 AM and at the Bear Lake trailhead by 4:00 – another long approach in the dark. Except for an occasional "bear warning" we walked quietly for an hour or so until dawn slowly started to illuminate the trail and we could see glimpses of our objective high above us and to our left. Eventually we veered off of the trail in the direction of Notchtop and followed a faint climbers trail past a series of small mountain lakes. We stopped at the last lake, directly below the approach gulley and the rather imposing summit of Notchtop, to have a bite to eat and rest before tackling the steep gulley. It was shaping up to be a beautiful day. The sky was blue and the morning temperature was a pleasant 50 or so degrees.

As we ascended the gulley another pair of climbers caught up with us. They had plans to climb a more direct and more difficult route which started close to where our route started. Austin had no problem scrambling up the gulley but after a few hundred feet I was grunting and groaning. I blamed it on old age. I really didn't feel old though and I often remind myself that I do things that only a small percentage of the general population could or would do, let alone the subset of the population in the 50+ age category. Climbing guidebooks are often vague about the details of climbs and that is particularly true of descriptions of alpine climbs. Guidebook authors often remark that they don't want to take all of the adventure out of the experience for their readers. Our guide called for veering right out of the gulley onto an upward sloping grassy ledge which would lead to the start of the technical climbing. The implication was that "it would be obvious." Such things rarely are. Once we gained a better perspective of the higher section of the tower three distinct ledges came into view, all of which generally satisfied the vague description in the guide. We opted for the third and highest of the three, reasoning that if the climb started out lower we would just connect with it but that if we started lower and the route didn't start until higher, we could find ourselves in way over our heads in terrain that isn't part of the 5.4 Spiral Route.

    As we exited the gulley onto the ledge we encountered the other climbing party again, roping up and getting ready to start out on the route they had chosen. This reinforced our belief that we were on the right ledge. We continued past them on the ledge, which narrowed from maybe 30 feet wide at its start down to a few inches at its terminus. We opted to rope up at the point where it was about 8 feet wide. We dropped our packs and retrieved harnesses, gear and ropes. After a short break I took the first lead out onto the narrowing ledge. The wall was curved so it was impossible to see more than 15 or 20 feet ahead. Below my feet was a drop-off of maybe 500 feet to a rocky slope and a snowfield. It was a bit intimidating but very exhilarating. I crept sideways on the diminishing ledge until there was no ledge, only handholds and footholds. Thankfully there were many of them and they were big and easy to use. There were plenty of places to place gear to which I attached my rope for protection in the event of a fall. I wasn't completely sure where to begin going up but came across a crack system in the rock wall that looked promising.

    I could have continued directly up but sharp turns in the rope create rope drag, meaning it is difficult to pull the rope along with you as you ascend. So as not to create too much rope drag I set up an anchor and belayed Austin across the 40 feet or so I had covered. He agreed that the terrain above looked promising and fun. I led the next pitch as well and climbed until I reached another small ledge with an alcove above it, maybe 80 feet above the last belay. Austin climbed up to meet me. We were both having a great time. We were all alone on a big rock wall on a beautiful day. I took the next pitch too and climbed until the 200 foot rope would allow me to go no further. I had reached a large grassy ledge called The Meadow. I belayed Austin up to the sunny perch which offered a spectacular view of Rocky Mountain National Park and Estes Park down below.

    We gathered our gear and hiked about 100 yards up and right along the huge grassy platform until we reached another section of steep rock which was supposed to lead to the notch that separates Notchtop from the main Continental Divide ridgeline. We couldn't really see the top from there but guessed that there were two more pitches. Austin took the next lead, about 40 feet up to a ledge. The down side to climbing east faces in the Rockies is that it is impossible to see weather approaching from the west. As Austin took off on the final pitch we noticed clouds floating by above us. I was eager to top out so we could see what the western sky had in store. The last pitch was by far the most difficult. It had one crux move that utilized a finger lock in a crack that I would probably call 5.9. Austin actually went around it, choosing instead an even more difficult face move. As he approached the belay at the notch the clouds became darker and more ominous but there were still huge gaps that revealed blue sky. I could not see any rain but we still had no sight line to the west.

It seemed to take Austin a long time to set up the anchor and put

Austin leads a pitch high on Notchtop

me on belay. Once on belay I cruised up the pitch as quickly as I could and joined him at the anchor. He had set it up about 10 feet below the notch for some reason so I still had to scamper up to the notch and belay him to that point. Ten feet doesn't sound like much but all of those transitions take time. Meanwhile the sky grew more ominous and I could hear the rumble of thunder in the distance. From the notch we scrambled up a ledge and gulley that led to the true summit. The ledge sloped steeply toward the edge of the cliff and was covered with loose stones. The little gulley took us to the top of Notchtop. To our left was a rappel station for the first of three 200 foot rappels according to the route beta we had gotten from the CMS guides. To our right was the true summit. From here we could see exactly how bad the situation had become. It was probably only around noon, a bit early for thunderstorms but certainly not unheard of. The sky to our west was black and we could see streaks of rain – downpours – not far off. Lightening was pummeling peaks to our west. We didn't have much time to get down to a safer position.

We didn't even bother to walk the 20 feet to tag the true summit. Instead I set up our first rappel as quickly as I could without compromising safety. I wasn't overly thrilled with the loops of perlon rope that had been left there as a rappel anchor. They looked a bit old and weathered. It would have taken a few precious extra minutes to retrieve webbing from my pack and add another redundant layer to the anchor. I tugged on them and inspected them and decided they would do. I took a quick glance at the handwritten diagram of the rappel sequence that one of the guides had given me the day before and rapped off first. There were supposed to be fairly new stainless steel bolted anchors a ways below us. How far below us I was not sure. Our rappel ropes were 200 feet long but it was nearly 600 feet down to the ledge where we had started climbing. I expected to find the anchors for the second rappel within the first hundred feet. After 100 feet I started to worry. By now it was raining lightly and the sound of thunder was close, within a mile or so by my estimation.

I rappelled almost to the end of my ropes and was very concerned. I had obviously missed the anchors. It turns out they are only about 40 feet below the initial anchor and off a bit to the right. I had been looking over my left shoulder as I rappelled down and didn't see them. Austin saw them on his way down. Fortunately for us someone else had made the same mistake – apparently years before. I was within 10 feet of the end of my rappel ropes when I saw a tattered piece of webbing wrapped around a large free standing rock flake which was leaning against the main wall. A single carabiner was attached to it. Obviously someone had used it to rappel. The webbing looked worn and there was only one strand. I had more webbing in my pack but I had no gear to set up a temporary anchor - Austin had the rack – and there was no ledge to stand on. Reluctantly I clipped into the webbing. I bounce-tested it a few times before disconnecting myself from the rope and shouting "off rappel." I hung there on that single strand of webbing as the intensity of the rain increased and the thunder grew louder. Austin appeared within a few minutes. He was eager to get off of that summit where he could see lightning strikes about every thirty seconds and wind-driven rain had soaked all of his clothes. I'm not sure why he hadn't put on his rain jacket but he was still shivering when he reached me at the improvised rappel station.

   As he approached the hanging belay I was attached to he looked at me like I was crazy and said "really?" "Oh shit." I said that I had obviously missed the bolted anchor. He replied: "I know. I saw it about 40 feet below the summit and about 20 feet to the right of your line." As I mentioned I had been looking over my left shoulder when I should have looked to the right. Sometimes bolts blend in with the color of the rock and can be difficult to see, depending on one's angle and the available light. Due to the clouds and rain our lighting conditions were less than optimal. "Anyway" I said. "This will have to do. Hopefully we can get back to the intended line and find the next real rappel station. Clip this thing and ease your weight onto it gently."

    He did that and I proceeded to pull our rappel rope. In climbing as with many endeavors bad things tend to happen at the worst possible time – Murphy's Law. This was the perfect time for Murphy to strike, and he did. The very end of our rappel rope jammed into a constriction about 20 feet above our heads as it fell down. We tugged on it but were unable to free it. We couldn't go further down until we recovered the end of the rope – at least not without cutting 20 feet or so off of the rope. By now the rock wall was wet, the most difficult and miserable obstacle to climbing. In addition we had no way of knowing how difficult the climbing above us would be since it was not part of our route. It didn't look that hard but it is difficult to evaluate such things from the perspective we had. Austin is by far the stronger climber between the two of us. I asked him to tie in to the end of the rope we had. I put him on belay and sent him up the wall to recover the other end of the rope.

    Fortunately the climbing was well within his range. He estimated it at easy 5.10 – but wet, which made it harder. When he reached the jammed rope he found a highly improbable cause for the jam. As the rope snaked down through a constriction a small pebble had dropped into the constriction with the rope, pinching it tight. The harder we pulled, the tighter the pebble pinched the rope. He quickly recovered the end of the rope and climbed back to our improvised rappel station. Almost as soon as I moved off of that scary rap station I saw the next rap station – maybe

40 feet below us and 20 feet off to our right – two shiny new stainless steel rappel anchors bolted to the wall. I was happy to see them. We were so focused on the task at hand that we really tuned out the storm that raged around us. I do remember one lightning strike that was followed immediately by one of the loudest claps of thunder I have ever heard, followed by the echo of that clap of thunder off of the surrounding rock walls. I suspect that lightning strike hit the peak we had just rappelled from. Within ten minutes we were back on the ledge we had started from and the worst of the storm had passed over us. The rain was easing up.

We were relieved to have survived our encounter with the storm – and my routefinding error – but it was hardly time to celebrate. We still had to negotiate that steep – and now wet – gulley and then hike five miles back to the trailhead. It took us nearly as long to go down the gulley as it had to ascend it. We had to be very careful because of the slippery wet rock. Once we got down to the series of lakes we turned on the afterburners and fast walked all the way back to the car. Now it was time to celebrate. We headed off to Estes Park's well known Smokin' Dave's BBQ and Taphouse for a feast.

Austin had indulged my itch for alpine climbing for a few days and had really had enough. He said there really wasn't anything else he wanted to do in Colorado that summer so we decided to pack up and head home the next day. I got up early and packed the car. About 9:00 I woke Austin up and we hit the road for yet another long day in the car. We drove all the way to Mt. Vernon, Illinois that day, arriving around midnight. We were both pretty beat so we stopped and got a hotel room for about 7 hours of sleep. That hotel, a Holiday Inn, has been a regular stop on my fairly frequent trips back and forth since. Mt. Vernon is about 80 miles east of St. Louis, which is roughly the halfway point between Richmond and Boulder. The next day we drove the rest of the way to Richmond. Austin was ready to start his senior year in high school and I was ready to start training for my second half-marathon.

Austin climbs through very steep terrain at the New River Gorge

Chapter 24

Growing Up and Moving On

**Various Locations
Fall, 2010 – Spring, 2011**

*I*n November I shaved nearly 20 minutes off of my half-marathon time from the previous year – about a minute and a half per mile. It was much better than I expected and I was ecstatic. I even ran it faster than one of my younger buddies who had trained for it as well. I felt great and knew I was in the best shape of my life – even better than when I ran track and played soccer in high school. Of course staying fit, at least staying near your peak, is at least as hard as getting there in the first place. My fitness level and my weight both wax and wane. I pretty much accept that it is inevitable and try to stay as fit as I can.

That fall Austin went to the New River Gorge for the first time without me. He went with a young climbing buddy who had recently graduated from Dartmouth and who is one of the two or three strongest climbers in Richmond. He came back having sent[1] Super-Mario, a 5.13a, on his second try. It was his first ascent of a 5.13. Austin also went back to Houndears that fall and this time he placed third in the men's advanced category. He was thrilled and I was very happy for him. He was training for his final year of competition in the USA Climbing youth categories and that year he decided to compete more seriously in the bouldering series which begins in the fall and culminates in a national championship in February.

    Austin performed well in the local bouldering comps and qualified to go to nationals in Boulder in February. By then he had decided for sure that Boulder (CU) was where he wanted to go to college so we were excited to visit once again. His mother had never seen the campus and decided to travel to Boulder as well to see Austin compete and to see the school he had picked. Austin trained hard for that competition. He was definitely stronger than he had ever been. Unfortunately he experienced something called a flash pump on his first of four qualifying problems. A flash pump happens when the muscles of the forearm become engorged with lactic acid and the blood cannot remove it and replace it with oxygenated blood quickly enough. When it happens it becomes very difficult, even impossible, to hold on to climbing holds. The phenomenon typically occurs when a climber fails to adequately warm up prior to climbing hard but sometimes occurs without explanation. Austin had warmed up properly but, as a result of the flash pump, performed poorly on the final three problems. He did not qualify to advance to the semi-finals.

---

1   To "send" a route is to climb it from bottom to top with no falls and no resting on the rope.

We still enjoyed our long weekend in Boulder, sampling some of the terrific restaurants on the Pearl Street Mall and touring around town. I even slipped away for a day up in Estes Park and a hike in the snow in Rocky Mountain National Park up to one of the alpine lakes.

Back in Richmond it was time to train for and compete in the spring competition series – the sport climbing series – and wait to hear from CU. Austin was accepted to CU in March. He finished 2nd at regionals and 1st at divisionals. Nationals was held once again at the now one year old gym in Atlanta, Stone Summit. Austin didn't want to travel out west with me that year. He was working at Peak Experiences and wanted to spend his free time with his buddies before he headed off to college in August.

By now I had pretty much given up on marketing my consulting practice and was thinking of myself as retired – or at least semi-retired. In January Peak Experiences asked me if I would be interested in teaching their lead climbing classes. I agreed and enjoyed passing along these skills to newer climbers. It was also a great opportunity to meet new climbers at the gym, some of whom I climb with now and then, both in the gym and occasionally in West Virginia. I taught about two classes each month for a while. Billy, my climbing partner from years before, also signed on as an instructor.

A friend of mine who is a "high pointer" had plans to climb Granite Peak that summer. A high pointer is a person who ascends to the high point of each of the fifty states. Granite Peak is the high point of the state of Montana. In many states attaining the high point is not a very big deal but in some states - Oregon, Washington, California, Colorado, Wyoming and Alaska come to mind – it is no small undertaking. The biggest by far is Denali (Mt. McKinley). At 20,320 feet it is the tallest summit in North America and, due its extreme northern latitude and absence of Sherpas, some say a more challenging feat than Everest. Among the fifty US high points many say Granite Peak is second only to Denali, even though it is not as tall or as technically challenging as some of the summits to its west which require snow and ice climbing skills. We decided to team up and do a climbing and hiking tour of eastern Colorado to acclimatize then head up to Montana to climb Granite then maybe climb a bit in Wyoming on the way home.

Austin was to drive to Boulder separately with his roommate, also from Richmond, and his "stuff" for college. I would meet up with him and his mom who was flying out from Richmond to help him move into his dorm. My summer plans were in place, and for the first time in many years did not include climbing with my son.

This was Austin's senior year in high school and he had performed well academically – not a gifted scholar but respectable grades, including a couple of honors/AP classes. Austin had also avoided any significant "trouble" along the way. He had pretty much been the child every parent hopes for – polite, responsible and well-behaved. This year though, like many teenagers, he tried a few "unapproved" recreational activities and "bent" the rules his mother and I had established. We were hopeful that these incidents were isolated and just "typical" teenage behavior. Nevertheless his mother and I were both concerned.

On Memorial Day weekend I drove to West Virginia

where I met Bill, who now lives in Johnson City, Tennessee and his friend Adam, who lives in Bowling Green, Kentucky, for three days of climbing at the New River Gorge and two days at Seneca Rocks. Bill had met Adam when he lived in Bowling Green before moving to Johnson City. Bill is about ten years younger than me and Adam is nearly 20 years younger than Bill. Bill had been one of Adam's climbing mentors, just as he had been for me. Having started climbing in his 20's though, Adam had far more promise as a climber than I ever did. Adam proved to be very strong and had impressive stamina on a rock wall. He was working hard on the "head game" associated with leading difficult rock – especially on gear (trad climbing).

While the New River Gorge is best known for its bolted sport climbing, there are probably just as many trad routes there. We climbed exclusively trad routes on this excursion. Our days there were extremely hot – daytime highs over 90 degrees – with high humidity. Heat and humidity are not the best conditions for climbing. Since both Adam and Bill are capable of leading 5.10 and harder on gear I was basically happy to let them lead routes and establish a top rope for me to have a go at them. That way I didn't have to work as hard or risk scary lead falls. It also provided Adam with a great opportunity to test his limits.

After a few days at the New, we drove over to Seneca Rocks. The temps had cooled a bit by the time we got there. As you may recall Seneca climbing is exclusively trad – and the crag is known for its "old school" ratings. We climbed a few of the classic routes at Seneca with Bill and Adam doing most of the leading. In fact I think I only led two pitches the whole time we were there. If I haven't

Bill, Adam and Manson (left to right) at Seneca Rocks

mentioned this before I am overdue in saying that climbing is a dangerous sport. While anyone who does it for a while – outdoors in particular – knows someone who has been seriously injured or killed, I am always surprised by how few climbing accidents there actually are each year. That is a real tribute to the rigor applied to safety measures by most members of the climbing community. That said we've all had our share of close calls. It was on this trip that I had perhaps my closest call in 13 years of climbing. Bill had led a traversing pitch near the top of a ridgeline climb on a somewhat chossy wall at the southern pillar of the crag. Chossy essentially means loose and/or friable. Friable means breakable – not solid. I went second on the pitch and as I approached the belay that Bill had set up perhaps ten feet above me, a hand hold broke off of the wall in my hand which caused me to fall.

Normally falling in a toprope situation like this would be no big deal. This time however when the weight of my body loaded a piece of gear Bill had used to set up the anchor the piece literally broke a cinderblock-sized chunk of rock out of the wall. The chunk crashed straight down onto my head where it broke into two pieces and plummeted 200 feet to the ground. Fortunately there was no one down there at the time – and fortunately I was wearing a helmet. I feel certain that if I had not been wearing it I would not be here to tell this story. It is also fortunate that Bill built a solid and redundant anchor with three pieces of gear. The other two held and saved both of us from a fast trip to the ground 200 feet below. I was slightly dazed but unhurt by the incident. Nevertheless I sat out the next route. An hour or so later I was ready to get back on the horse and led the first pitch of our next route.

As always I enjoyed Bill's company and was delighted to meet Adam. We agreed that we needed to get together again for more climbing. As I drove back to Richmond I was eager to make that happen. About a month later Bill went to Peru on a climbing and mountaineering trip with his friend John. John had just climbed Denali. In fact I believe he was on Denali while we were in West Virginia. They invited me to join them in Peru but after much deliberation I declined. I was concerned that they did not seem to have a very firm plan for the trip – no specific objectives in mind and no reservations for a place to stay while not on a mountain. Bill later reported that they had a good trip but it wasn't something he wanted to do again. He had lost his appetite for remote, high altitude mountaineering. Bill has knee and back problems so it is not hard to understand how he could find mountaineering trying. In fact every year for at least three years now he has claimed to be retired from climbing – only to return when one of his buddies organizes a climbing trip. In fact as I write this in the spring of 2012 I recently invited Bill and Adam on my 2012 trip to the Rockies. That has evolved into a (now planned) trip to the Bugaboos, a spectacular climbing venue in British Columbia, Canada, that entails both mountaineering (snowy glacier approaches) and rock climbing on striking granite spires towering high above the glaciers. I really look forward to climbing with both Bill and Adam again. We met that May (2012) in Kentucky for a weekend of rock climbing in a place that Adam is developing. Despite high heat and humidity and an abundance of ticks and chiggers we had a great time.

    July, 2011 rolled around and Austin and I drove to Atlanta for his final youth national championship. I can't speak for Austin but it was an emotional time for me. We had spent so much time together as he grew up, much of it climbing, and that was about to come to an end. Climbing had provided the venue for us to build a strong relationship, as father and son, as climbing partners and as friends. This was perhaps our last such trip together. Many of our friends commented on our years of climbing and congratulated Austin on making it to nine consecutive national championships. A few asked me how I felt. I had to choke back tears a few times. Austin finished 21st. Even though that's not far from where he had finished in recent years he was still disappointed. We enjoyed the rest of the competition and camaraderie with other climbers, parents, coaches and USAC officials. At the award ceremony on Sunday Austin was honored for his many trips to the national championship and his dedication to the sport. Tears streamed down my face, just as they are now as I write this. Austin had never made it to a world championship. I was sad for him. At the same time he had secured a sponsorship with one of the climbing shoe manufacturers and planned on "going pro." He was ready to move on.

    Going pro means different things in different sports. In climbing it can mean competing as a professional for prize money, earning money from sponsors, often climbing new and difficult routes which are covered by the climbing media, or it can mean making a living as a climbing guide, instructor or even as a guidebook author. Austin intended to compete for money, although the kind of money that is offered at pro climbing comps isn't enough to live on, let alone get wealthy. In fact very few climbers make any sort of decent living just by climbing. There simply isn't enough sponsorship or prize money for that. That may change if and when climbing ever becomes an Olympic sport. The financial success of many sports and athletes is impacted greatly by being televised. Efforts have been under way to get climbing into the Olympics for a number of years and organizers are hopeful that it may become a reality in the 2020 Olympics. Even if that happens it remains to be seen if climbing will ever become a popular spectator sport. Climbers are small percentage of the population and non-climbers have a hard time appreciating what they are looking at. There's not much "action" from the perspective of the average spectator, at least not until the climber falls, and it is hard for someone who has never tried it to appreciate how difficult it is to climb the more difficult routes.

    Austin hoped to perform well at the University Of Colorado Leeds School Of Business, work part time at one of the rock climbing gyms in Boulder (Movement), and compete as a pro at several comps throughout the coming school year and beyond. While we were in Atlanta at nationals the head coach from Movement whom we had known since she was a youth competitor herself offered Austin a job as a coach. Things were really falling in place for him.

Chapter 25

Highs and Lows in the Rockies

Colorado, Montana, Wyoming
August, 2011

*M*y high pointer friend – Susanne - and I left Richmond in early August and drove to Boulder. We climbed there for a couple of days, taking our time acclimatizing to altitude, then drove up to Estes Park.

Estes is about 3,000 feet higher than Boulder. We rented a small cabin for a few days and spent them hiking and climbing in the park. We actually did more hiking than climbing, mostly up to 12 or 13 thousand feet. Susanne was fairly new to rock climbing and had never climbed trad or multi-pitch before this trip so we stayed well within our climbing ability. We had a terrific trip up Magical Chrome Plated Semi-Automatic Enema Syringe, my third time up the route.

After about five days we packed up and headed back to Boulder where I met up with Austin and helped him move into his dorm. CU has a two day orientation

LEFT Above tree line in Rocky Mountain National Park

The author leads the way on the Third Flatiron near Boulder, CO

for parents that runs in parallel with freshman orientation. I participated in that while Austin got settled in and attended his orientation. Susanne toured Boulder, did a bit of hiking and rented a mountain bike for some riding. After a couple of days it was time to say goodbye to Austin. I had thought about that moment many times, trying to imagine how I would feel and trying to prepare for it. In the end there is no way to prepare. I was a mess. I was completely choked up, sobbing and teary-eyed. I couldn't even speak. Of course Austin showed no visible signs of emotion and said: "Dad, you're not going to do that are you?" I looked him in the eyes, hugged him, and choked out "I love you - be safe" then turned around and walked off. I was half way across the campus before the tears stopped.

The next day Susanne and I left early and drove to Montana. Granite Peak is in south central Montana close to the border with Wyoming and just north of Yellowstone National Park. It is about 80 miles southwest of Billings. The closest towns are Absarokee (pronounced Ab-sor-kee) and Red Lodge. They are both pretty small but each has a variety of motels and B&B's. Red Lodge is the gateway to a popular winter ski resort. Camping is also available close to both of the popular trailheads for the mountain. At 12,807 feet Granite Peak is not one of the higher summits in the US. Among state high points it ranks only tenth. But it has a long approach with considerable elevation gain and lots of off trail hiking, rock-hopping, snow-field crossings, a bit of technical rock near the summit, and even a snow-bridge crossing. There are two popular approaches, one from the north and one from the east. The two trails converge at about 10,500 feet on the Froze-to-Death Plateau. The trail from the north ascends steeply up 26 switch-backs while the trail from the east is a bit more mellow, spreading the elevation gain out over a greater distance. We chose the steeper and slightly shorter northern approach.

    We didn't arrive in Absarokee until about 10:00 at night. We had rented a room in a house – essentially a B&B – but without the breakfast. We turned in as soon as we got there. The next day we drove around and explored the area. The literature said it could be difficult to find the trailhead, especially in the early morning darkness, so we drove there to make sure we knew where we would be going early the next morning. It ended up being pretty straightforward but there is a long stretch, maybe 20 miles, of dirt/gravel road. Once we were confident we could find our trailhead we drove over to Red Lodge to look around. Red Lodge is a bit "touristy." The Main Street looks like that of a lot of old western towns that cater to tourists - wall to wall shops, restaurants, hotels, art galleries and real estate offices. On the way back to Absarokee we stopped at a local landmark – the Grizzly Bar. The Grizzly Bar is a surprisingly good restaurant in the middle of nowhere. It claims to be in Roscoe, Montana but as far as I could tell it is the only thing in Roscoe.

Susanne is a petite woman but she is an accomplished athlete and outdoors-person. At the time she had ascended 47 of the state summits. Only Granite Peak, Katahdin (Maine), and Denali remained. Obviously she had become quite experienced in basic mountaineering, having ascended Mt. Whitney (California), Gannet (Wyoming) and both Mt. Hood (Oregon) and Rainier (Washington), along with a host of other peaks. Her nemesis was bearing the extreme pack weights typically associated with multi-day trips up mountains. With climbing and camping gear, food, fuel and water a mountaineering pack can easily weigh 60 pounds or more. I'd guess that Susanne weighs barely 100 pounds. Fifty pounds represents 50% of her body weight. She likes to keep her pack weight under 40 pounds and preferably under 30. As I've mentioned before, porters are pretty much unheard of in the US but Susanne had done quite a bit of research and had located a climbing guide who was willing to work as a porter for our trip up Granite.

Guiding on most mountains throughout the world is governed by some government entity, usually a park service or wilderness management entity. Almost all of them limit the number of guide services that can operate on their mountains and require them to have permits. There are two guide services that have permits for Granite, Jackson Hole Mountain Guides based in Jackson, WY and a local guide service that is all but defunct. We did not need or want a guide for our attempt, and we certainly didn't want to pay for a guide when all we really wanted was a porter. As far as we could tell there were no rules governing porters on Granite and Susanne negotiated a deal with a guy named Juan. Juan guides in South America in the southern hemisphere summer and in Montana in the northern hemisphere summer. Susanne had negotiated a fee for Juan to carry about 20 pounds of gear for us to our base camp and then back down two days later.

We were up at 3:00 AM the next day and at the trailhead by 4:00. As we pulled in to the parking lot there were several cars parked but no sign of life. We started to get our packs and gear out and before long we heard a car door close across the parking area. A headlamp flickered and a tall, lanky figure approached in the darkness. Juan had arrived late the night before and slept for a few hours in his car. He said he wasn't feeling well and wanted to collect our gear, get a few more hours of sleep and hike up the trail and catch up with us on Froze-to-Death Plateau. That sounded fine with us, though Susanne was a bit concerned about the rendezvous. We gave Juan our tent, ice axes, crampons, rope and climbing gear, shouldered our packs and headed off in the darkness. It was about 4:30 AM.

The first few miles of the approach are pretty mellow – a developed trail along a stream. The stream leads to its source, a dammed lake named Mystic Lake. In addition to the outlet stream the lake feeds a small hydroelectric plant located at the trailhead by way of a large pipe that parallels the trail. The sun was beginning to rise as we crested the dam and began our traverse around the lake. After another quarter mile the trail splits and we turned sharply left toward the mountain, or more accurately toward Froze-to-Death Plateau. Pretty soon we were negotiating the infamous switchbacks. One of the online guides we had read referred to them as "the switchbacks from hell." We counted the switchbacks out loud as we made each turn. I enjoyed measuring our progress this way and, at our reasonable pace, the ascent was not as grueling as I had anticipated. I had actually spent many hours on a step mill (Stairmaster) with a backpack loaded with 50 pounds of weights in the months leading up to this trip in preparation for Granite. It was a beautiful day and the scenery was spectacular. We gradually gained higher and higher vantage points from which to view Mystic Lake and other smaller lakes. We made good progress and reached a clearing that marked tree line and the beginning of Froze-to-Death Plateau around noon. We walked over to where the trail converged with the one from the other trailhead. We dropped our packs there to eat lunch and wait for Juan.

We had set a fairly leisurely pace and knew that any climbing guide would be able to go much faster, even with a heavier burden. But after about 40 minutes there was no sign of Juan. Susanne's worries grew but I was sure he'd show up. I convinced her to move further up the plateau. I could see that we could go another mile or so and still have a vantage of where the trail popped up out of the trees onto the plateau. The plateau is really more of a ramp. It is about five miles long and nearly a mile wide in places. There is no real trail and much of the terrain involves rock-hopping on often unstable boulders and some interesting snowfield crossings. The edges of the plateau drop off steeply. From the convergence of the trails to the end of the plateau, just below Tempest Peak, there is an elevation gain of about 1,500 feet but the rock-hopping makes it seem much more strenuous than 1,500 feet would suggest.

We began the slog up the plateau and stopped at a rocky perch about a mile further along - still no sign of Juan. I was ready to continue but Susanne didn't want to go further up the mountain until she knew we would have our tent. We waited perhaps an hour before a lone figure popped up over the edge of the plateau and made a beeline directly up the plateau – he was moving fast and in a more direct line than we had taken. We set out on a traversing course to intercept him and after about 20 minutes our paths converged. By now it was around 2:00 PM. It was indeed Juan. He said he had continued to have a bit of stomach distress and left the car later than he expected. He had vomited a few times on the trail and stopped to rest each time. When we first saw him moving up the plateau we would never have guessed that he felt any less than 100%.

It is possible to camp just about anywhere on the plateau but there are established tent sites at several locations – near the beginning of the plateau, about 2/3 of the way to the top, about a half mile below the top and at the very top. Over the years climbers have built rocky walls that protect tent sites from prevailing westerly winds. There are no trees or any natural wind blocks so it can really howl up there. Our goal was the top of the plateau at 12,000 feet.

Susanne moves cautiously on unstable terrain and caution takes time. By 5:00 we were still about a mile and a half below our goal for the day but we were tired and ready to call it a day. We found a tent site and set up camp. Our freeze-dried dinners tasted like gourmet meals after all of that exertion and our sleeping pads felt like mattresses. When the sun set we were treated to a dazzling black sky infused with millions of stars. The temperature dropped quickly once the sun set so it wasn't long before we were ready to climb inside our warm down sleeping bags. I set my alarm for 4:00 AM.

It was still dark and cold – mid-20's - when I crawled out of the tent but the moon had risen during the night. It cast an eerie moonscape

Suzanne at our camp on Granite Peak

glow on the rocky terrain. We didn't talk much as we prepared coffee and a light breakfast. My standard breakfast in the backcountry is instant grits and string cheese along with hot coffee. By 5:00 we had secured camp and shouldered our packs. I had all of the climbing gear – a rope and a light rack as well as a pair of crampons. We both carried extra layers, food, water and an ice axe. I had brought along a new lightweight "summit pack" to try out. It is much smaller than the 65 liter pack I had used to reach camp but it has no real structure and thus doesn't manage weight very well. Loaded, the pack probably weighed 30 pounds - really more than it was designed for. Susanne's pack probably weighed 20 pounds.

Juan was still asleep. He had no "duties" that day. We left camp and picked our way up the seemingly endless boulderfield by the light of our headlamps. We hugged the right side of the plateau because we didn't want to miss the exit onto the right shoulder of the plateau that led to the next section of the climb. About a mile up the plateau the sun began to rise and we were joined by a herd of mountain goats that followed us all the way to the top of the plateau. It turned out that our exit from the plateau is well marked by an enormous cairn[1] – and it is directly adjacent to the high camp, home to numerous tent sites, each surrounded by a wall of rocks constructed long ago by other climbers. There were no other tents there however on this morning. It appeared that we were the only people up high on the mountain.

It was here that we got our first actual glimpse of Granite Peak. Up until now it was hidden behind the upper reaches of Froze-to-Death Plateau. I must admit that it was more than a little bit intimidating. Our vantage point provided a dramatic view of the very steep north face of the mountain, a nearly vertical drop of thousands of feet to boulderfields and a lake. We could also see the striking east ridge which would provide our approach to the higher section of the mountain where we would veer left to the south face and several hundred feet of relatively easy technical rock to reach the summit.

I mentioned earlier that Froze-to-Death Plateau is bordered by steep drop-offs on both sides. The exit from the plateau near the top is only slightly less steep. It is a dangerous slope covered by loose rocks and boulders and the occasional snowfield, depending on the season. There is no trail but the route is marked by cairns, many of which are hard to see from any distance. They simply blend in

---

[1] A cairn is a pile of rocks created by hikers and climbers to mark the route or turning points in the route. They range from small, less than a foot tall, to enormous, eight or more feet tall.

with all of the other rocks. The route traverses and gradually descends the scary slope over the course of perhaps a mile to reach a saddle between Tempest Mountain, which is essentially the summit of Froze-to-Death Plateau, and Granite Peak, a mile or so to the west. If we thought the boulders of Froze-to-Death Plateau were treacherous, this slope was downright frightening. I am fairly agile and move well in the mountains, especially downhill, but this slope required every bit of my attention. We finally reached the saddle where we took a break for food and water.

    While we sat at the saddle another party, a father and son, passed us and headed into the steep traverse ahead. I was hoping to get a sense of the route by watching them but they disappeared around an outcropping within a few minutes and we never saw them again. We ventured down into a class 4 traverse which led to our first steps on the actual flank of Granite Peak. From there we had a few choices. We could either angle left and head for a large and fairly steep snowfield or angle right and skirt the snowfield to the right along the very exposed ridge. The ridge appeared both steep and loose so we opted for the snowfield. We still had to scramble up some very steep and in places very loose rock to reach the snowfield. Once we got there we discovered that it was still frozen very hard from the cold night before. It was so hard that I couldn't even kick steps into the surface with my stiff hiking boots. This was really crampon terrain but we only had one pair between us. We decided to let Susanne use the crampons and I would try to kick steps when I could and move cautiously when I couldn't. I had my ice axe ready in case I fell and started to slide back toward the rocks. Once I was about 30 feet onto the snow (really more like ice) and Susanne was about 10 feet out another climber appeared off to our right on the rocky bypass. He was headed down. He called to us that the route he was on seemed faster and safer than the snowfield. Apparently he had gone up that way earlier in the morning after experimenting with the snowfield just as we were.

We decided to heed his advice. I was relieved to make it back to the rocks. The descending climber was soon out of sight. He must have slept at the high camp and packed up his tent and stowed it in the rocks before setting off early that morning. From this point the route ascends steeply over class 3 and short sections of class 4 rocky terrain about 1,000 feet to a ridgeline that traverses in from the left then descends to another saddle. That saddle is a permanent snow bridge, essentially a narrow snow covered ridge with very steep drops of over 1,000 feet on each side and perhaps 30 feet across. This is one of the highlights of the Granite Peak climb. Unfortunately I never saw it. We were a couple of hundred feet below the traversing ridgeline and moving slow. It was well past noon and there were dark clouds skirting across the sky from the west. We could not see the western sky because Granite Peak was in the way. We assessed the situation and opted to turn around.

As we arrived back at the saddle between Tempest and Granite Juan arrived – in shorts, tennis shoes and a tee shirt. He had a small fanny pack in which I presume he had a light rain layer. By now it was closing in on 2:00. Juan planned to cruise up and tag the summit. Mountain guides are a sturdy (and brave) bunch. We set out for camp. As we made our way carefully back across the steep, rocky slope ominous clouds skirted our position but it didn't rain. We could occasionally see lightening along neighboring summits and ridges. It was probably 5:00 when we got back to camp. Juan arrived shortly after us, having tagged the summit. Pretty soon thereafter a very large thunderstorm bore down on us and the skies opened up. Lightning and thunder were all around us. We retreated to our tents and waited out the downpour which lasted more than two hours. I own several tents. It turned out that this was the first time this particular tent had been subjected to a torrential downpour. It failed the test. Several of the seams leaked and Susanne and I found ourselves using a pack towel to sop up the water which we then squeezed out through the door of the tent. It was fairly miserable. As the rain eased up I dozed off and didn't awake until late that night.

I got up and climbed out of the tent to take a pee and check out the night sky. It did not disappoint – crystal clear with more stars than I can even imagine. I even saw a couple of shooting stars before I got chilly and crawled back into the tent.

The next day we took our time eating breakfast and breaking camp. It was another bluebird day. Susanne was tempted to take another shot at the summit but we had only hired Juan for three days and I wasn't really eager to retrace our steps so soon. It only took five or six hours to hike back out to the trailhead where we cracked open a few cold beers that we found in the car. Surprisingly some of the ice in our cooler had survived and the contents of the cooler were still pretty cold. As we sat at the trailhead and enjoyed the beer I noticed that Juan was missing parts of several of his fingers. I thought about asking him about it but never really felt like the timing was right. Later (as I was climbing Aconcagua in January 2012) I was told that he had spent an unplanned overnight on the steep south wall of Aconcagua earlier that year (2011) where he had suffered frostbite on several of his fingers.

Juan told us more about his work and his partner, Mike "Coop" Cooperstein. They operate a guide service in Montana during the northern hemisphere summer and another guide service in Argentina (and throughout South America) in the southern hemisphere summer. Juan encouraged me to look into their guided climb up Aconcagua. He said it would be the perfect next step for someone with my mountaineering experience. It sounded very tempting and I decided to look into it. From there we drove back to the Grizzly Bar for a terrific early dinner. Afterward we parted ways with Juan and headed back to Absarokee, looking forward to sleeping in real beds after two nights in the mountains.

The next day we got up early and drove down Beartooth Pass Highway into Wyoming and eventually into Yellowstone National Park. Our plan was to spend the night in Jackson, Wyoming and take on one of the non-technical summits in Grand Teton National Park the next day before driving back east. The Beartooth Pass Highway, which is closed in the winter, is a mountain road that twists and turns its way south and west from Red Lodge, Montana to Yellowstone. I'd give it high marks as a scenic drive. A driving tour of Yellowstone always makes for a pleasant day and this day was no exception. We saw several large herds of buffalo and a few moose as we made our way south through the park. We stopped for the obligatory eruption of Old Faithful Geyser and had lunch nearby then pressed on for GTNP and Jackson.

Once we arrived at Grand Teton National Park it was late afternoon but we stopped at the Exum Mountain Guides headquarters near Jenny Lake to have a look at the mountains and get a recommendation for our outing the next day. I was keen on Teewinot – the striking summit just east of the Grand Teton that Billy and I had attempted five years earlier. Actually Billy summited it. I attempted it and came up several hundred feet shy of the summit. The winter of 2011 had left much more snow in the mountains than usual though and the snowfield on which I had slipped five years earlier looked about twice as big from the valley as I had ever seen it. The guides at Exum confirmed that it was a substantially greater obstacle than in previous years. From the valley it looks steeper than it actually is too and Susanne was pretty intimidated by it. In the end we opted to hike up to the Lower Saddle (the saddle between the Grand and Middle Tetons) and possibly beyond to the Upper Saddle depending upon weather and time.

The decision made, we headed over to Dornan's, an outdoor cookout place in Moose, Wyoming with an incredible view of the Tetons where we enjoyed the sunset and a decent meal. Afterward we drove to Jackson and got a motel room for a couple of nights and turned in early.

The next morning we were up early yet again, this time around 3:00 AM. It was my birthday and I was eager to celebrate it by getting high on a mountain. We downed coffee and snacks and headed for the Garnet Canyon Trailhead at Lupine Meadows. By 4:00 we were hiking in the cool, dark, woods. The only sounds were those of our footsteps, the nearby creek and the clicking of my trekking poles. Susanne wasn't feeling well that day. Her stomach was unsettled. She tried some over-the-counter meds I keep in my pack and they didn't seem to do much good but she plugged on. Gradually her condition improved but she really didn't feel strong all day. We made our way into Garnet Canyon and past The Meadows then ascended past Spalding Falls to the Petzolt Caves. I had not been on this trail since 2003 and the upper part of the mountain looked somewhat unfamiliar – perhaps due to the unusually large snowpack that remained from the winter.

    Susanne felt that the direction I pointed out to gain the Lower Saddle could not possibly be right. It looked like it might be impossible to go much higher without encountering steep snow and/or technical rock. About the same time we spotted a hut about 800 feet above us and off to the right. I suspected that this might be the Jackson Hole Mountain Guides hut but I had never actually seen it before and was not certain. Susanne thought it must be the Exum Guides hut at the Lower Saddle. One rarely wins any sort of argument with Susanne, plus the side trip to the JHMG hut looked like an interesting diversion, so I agreed to go "exploring." There is supposed to be a faint side trail that ascends the rocky and steep slope to the JHMG hut and campsite but we never saw it, even once we got there and were able to look down. We scrambled off trail all the way up there which proved to be quite strenuous.

    There was no one there but we were able to replenish our water supply from a glacial runoff and we sat and ate lunch and enjoyed the view. In order to resume the trip to the Lower Saddle from there one actually has to descend back to the main trail. Again, there is supposed be another faint climbers trail down the backside of the "hill" that the

JHMG camp sits on leading back to the main trail but again I could not find it. At this point Susanne elected to head back down and I elected to push on to the Lower Saddle. As we parted ways she hollered out that she would meet me at the Caves – at least that's what I thought she said.

I rock-hopped down to the main trail and enjoyed the strenuous hike the rest of the way up to the Lower Saddle. It probably took me an hour or so. When I got there I was greeted by darkening skies that threatened to produce rain. I was also greeted by a party of climbers who had just come down from the summit of the Grand. They were an extended family and a friend or two, guided by Exum. The whole group, including their guides, were quite friendly. The guides knew some of the guides I had met on previous trips and were happy to pass along my regards to them. The "mom" of the group also turned out to be a birthday girl. Not only did we share a birthday, we were exactly the same age. We were born on the very same day in the very same year. Neither of us had ever met anyone else born on the same day. We hugged and took pictures. They were packing up to head back down the mountain and I needed to decide if I was going to go further or head down as well.

Birthday girl and boy

I wandered around up there – the views both to the east and to the west are spectacular – for a while as I assessed the weather and made note of the fact that

Susanne was waiting for me down below. I headed back down the trail, making really good time. It had been an excellent birthday celebration. Within an hour or so I was down to the giant rock near the Petzolt Caves. There was no sign of Susanne. I asked parties moving up the mountain if they had seen anyone fitting her description. She would have been hard to miss – a petite blond who had braided her hair into pigtails that day and wore a red baseball cap. No one had seen her. In my mind that meant that somehow she must still be up higher on the mountain. I started to ask descending parties if they had seen her and asked them to keep a look out for her as they went further down the mountain. I waited there for over an hour. Eventually I decided to head down and look for her further down the mountain. As soon as I donned my pack and traversed the first of dozens of switchbacks adjacent to Spalding Falls I heard someone call my name. It was of course Susanne, perhaps 100 feet below. One of the descending parties I had spoken with had encountered her down near The Meadows and told her that I was waiting for her at the Caves. She had headed back up to get me.

It turns out that when she announced that she would meet me earlier she had said she would meet me at The Meadows. I had misunderstood her. Anyway, all was well. It was still relatively early in the afternoon. The weather had improved and the sun was shining and we could easily hike out to the trailhead in four hours or so. The mountains are full of adventure – big and small – but I definitely recommend being clear about one's plans, especially when rendezvous are involved. A pleasant day in the mountains can turn into an epic pretty quickly.

Once back at the car we drove straight to our motel for a shower then headed out to a steak place Susanne had found out about. She was hankering for an elk steak and apparently this place is the only place in town that has them. I ordered a bison steak. Bison and buffalo are one in the same. Both of our meals were delicious. Susanne drank a couple of beers and I drank a couple of glasses of wine. She treated me for my birthday. It had been one of my best birthdays ever. It had also been a great trip and this marked the end of our adventure. Like most of my trips it had had its share of successes and failures. By then I had pretty much come to accept that failure is as much a part of mountaineering as success, maybe more. In each failure there is learning, about the mountain, about ourselves, about our decision-making, about weather, and of course acquiring new skills and honing existing ones. In fact I had stopped thinking of failure to reach a summit as failure at all. Success means getting home safely after an exciting and enjoyable experience punctuated by good decisions along the way, regardless of whether a summit was attained.

The next morning we were on the road by 7:00. After a quick breakfast in Jackson we headed south and then east through Wyoming where we were treated to a lovely view of the western slope of the Wind River Range as we drove parallel to it on highway 191. We broke the drive into three roughly 11 hour days of driving. Our first stop was Kearney, Nebraska and our second stop was good old Mt. Vernon, Illinois. We arrived in Richmond at the same time as Hurricane Irene. We encountered strong winds and heavy rain as we approached Richmond from the west. Upon arrival we discovered that the power was out. It remained that way at my house for over a week. I guess I didn't need to go to the mountains to find adventure.

The author on a wintery exploration of Longs Peak

Chapter 26

Rocky Starts and a Big Next Step

Virginia and Colorado
Fall, 2011 – December, 2011

As we drove back from Wyoming I thought about Austin settling in to his new life in college – so far from home. I was eager to get back to Boulder to see how he was doing and to spend more time in the mountains so I planned a trip out there for family weekend at the University of Colorado – the first weekend in October. It turned out that a big pro climbing comp – part of the World Cup Series and the first in the US in many years – was scheduled in Boulder the weekend after family weekend at CU. I decided to stay for 12 days. I could enjoy family weekend with Austin and maybe a bit of sport climbing, head up into the mountains for a few days in the backcountry, return to Boulder for the comp and more time with Austin then fly home. I hoped to knock out at least one more 14'er while I was there.

It wasn't long before Austin informed me that he had been "busted" by the school for drinking in his dorm room. Apparently the campus police had been called in for a noise complaint. That resulted in a warning letter, an alcohol "class" and other sanctions and put him on thin ice with the school. Shortly after that there was another incident involving alcohol in his room. This time the Boulder police were summoned and, in addition to ramifications with the school, Austin was charged with a "Minor in Possession" by the City of Boulder and had to go to court to face the music. His court date was scheduled for the week I was to be there. He was now in very deep water. In addition to other sanctions the school suspended him in abeyance. In essence he could continue to attend classes but even the tiniest infraction, including failure to abide by the sanctions and complete the assigned responsibilities would result in dismissal. Austin's mother and I were obviously deeply concerned. There was even discussion of pulling him out of school then – in the middle of the semester. Austin of course was convinced that he was doing the same things that "everyone else" was doing and that he had merely been the victim of bad luck. Nevertheless, he committed to complying with all of the sanctions and cleaning up his act. In reality, I also feel like he was doing the same things as a large number of first year college kids and, in particular, the group that he had "fallen in" with early in the semester. But those "things," and especially the frequency with which he participated were simply not acceptable to me.

 It is very difficult to influence a child who is living on their own, especially when they are 1,700 miles away. I grew increasingly concerned throughout the fall and was eager to get back to Boulder to assess firsthand how things were going. In the meanwhile, I revoked Austin's driving privileges. Of course that was on the honor system since he still had the keys and I was too far away to enforce the sanction.

Meanwhile I exchanged emails with Coop Cooperstein of Andes Mountain Guides and explored a January expedition to Aconcagua. It was not long before I committed to the trip, sending in my deposit and booking airfare to South America. Coop also gave me some suggestions on things to do while I was in Colorado.

I flew to Denver on the Wednesday before family weekend and took the shuttle bus to Boulder. It dropped me off only a few hundred yards from Austin's dorm. My plan was to "borrow" Austin's Xterra while I was there. I was not overjoyed to find the car filthy dirty and full of trash when I arrived. It also would not start due to a dead battery. Austin had left a cell phone charger plugged in without starting the vehicle. AAA to the rescue. Pretty soon I was checked in to a nearby motel and returned to campus to pick Austin and his roommate up for dinner. Austin fessed up that he had been lending the car to his roommate – something I had specifically forbidden before he ever went to school.

All in all though, the visit with Austin went well. We climbed in the local gyms a couple of times and at an outdoor sport climbing crag one day. We also attended the home football game. We visited a few of our favorite restaurants in Boulder and tried a couple of new ones. All the while I could not shake an uneasy feeling about his priorities. Our agreement was that he would get a part time job which, after seven weeks, he had failed to do, despite the job offer from the coach at Movement. He also did not seem very enthusiastic about academics – the main reason for being there. Finally, he really hadn't done any climbing since he had been there – except with me. Prior to going to Boulder Austin had been excited about advancing his climbing career. Boulder is really the center of the climbing world in the United States – in particular the competition climbing world. Many of the top pro climbers in the US live and train in Boulder. And of course Austin had secured the sponsorship with the climbing shoe manufacturer. I'm sure they expected him to compete. Now he seemed pretty ambivalent about all of it.

Navajo Peak

CU has a long standing reputation as one of the "top" party schools in the country. Based on everything I have heard and seen it is well deserved. That is not to say that the school embraces that reputation. In fact it appears that they do everything in their power to distance themselves from it and that they take underage drinking, intoxication and substance abuse very seriously. The truth is a student can elect to party to excess – or to get a fantastic education – at most any school in the country. The bigger the school, perhaps the bigger the opportunity for both.

    While I was in Colorado, I took a shot at Navajo Peak in the Indian Peaks Wilderness and Mt. Sneffels, way down in the southwest corner of the state. Indian Peaks Wilderness is a protected area about the size of Rocky Mountain National Park and adjacent to the park to the south. Depending upon the access point, one can drive there from Boulder in well under an hour. I got up early in Boulder, had breakfast at the local IHOP and parked my car at the trailhead for Navajo Peak by 6:00. It was still dark and my car was the only car in the lot. After a couple of hours on a gradually diminishing trail I had passed treeline and several high mountain lakes. It was a crisp clear autumn morning and the scenery was spectacular – made even more so by the changing (golden yellow) leaves of the Aspen trees. Eventually I reached the point where my route parted the trail. I hadn't seen another human being all morning. It was just me and the mountain. I tried to avoid thinking about Austin and just enjoy the day, but it wasn't easy. I noted that there was still a film of ice from the night before on the last lake I passed before heading up a snowfield and then a steep talus slope.

    My goal was to attain Navajo Peak by way of Airplane Gully. It is called that because the couloir (or gully) actually contains the remains of an airplane that crashed there in 1948. Navajo Peak is an attractive summit that resembles and upside down ice cream cone. It tops out at

203

13,409'. Airplane Gully ascends its eastern flank and deposits the climber in a saddle just south of the peak. The route is considered class 3 due to exposed and steep moves from the saddle up to the summit.

After crossing another large field of talus, I reached Airplane Gully. Immediately I began to see pieces of the wreckage – pretty surreal. The gully is steep and fairly loose with scree and talus of a wide range of sizes. It is wide at the bottom where rockfall fans out and narrows at it ascends. Higher up the gully I could see snow. I couldn't tell if it was left over from the previous winter or if it was a remnant of a snowfall from a week before. Either way I could tell that the upper reaches of the gully didn't see much if any direct sunlight this time of year. I trudged upward. It reminded me a bit of The Trough on Longs Peak. As the gully narrowed I reached the snowy section. I had not counted on this. In fact I had brought neither ice axe nor crampons with me. I pushed on, trying to kick steps in the snow and gain purchase on the exposed rock on the side of the gully. It was slow going and very tedious. My approach shoes have soft rubber soles which are great on rock but terrible on snow. The farther up I went the harder the snow became. In places it was literally ice from thawing and refreezing over the course of recent days and nights. It was very slippery and tenuous. Eventually the snow and ice got so scary that I resorted to climbing and traversing along the right side on fairly easy but steep rock. A slip anywhere here would have been very bad, likely fatal. Eventually I reached a ledge on the right side of the gully just below where the gully splits. The ledge actually was in the sun so it was free of snow and ice. I stopped there to eat lunch and contemplate the situation.

My route took the right fork at the split which incidentally is where the biggest concentration of airplane wreckage lies. Unfortunately the upper section was also shaded from the sun and appeared to be at least as treacherous as the section I had just climbed. Climbing further without crampons and an ice axe would be folly – and downclimbing it on the way out would be worse. Heck, downclimbing the part I had already ascended weighed heavily on my mind. I elected to call it a day and retreat.

Since I knew that I would be in the mountains alone on this trip I had purchased a device called a SPOT satellite transmitter which can send pre-formatted messages via satellite to a central monitoring station and on via email to anyone you chose. I fished the device out of my pack and sent the "I'm OK" message to record my location (GPS coordinates) and high point – just for posterity. Then I shouldered my pack for the trip down. I was more than a little bummed out to miss out on the best part of the climb – the class 3 scrambling to the summit.

It was cold in the shady gully but the day was beautiful and I enjoyed terrific vistas of the valley and glacial tarns below. I was eager to get back in the sunlight but knew I had to take my time and carefully place each step and hand as I backed my way down the steeper sections of the slippery gully. I basically retraced my steps from the ascent. As I reached the end of the snowy/icy section I looked down to see two other mountaineers ascending the gully. They were still a few hundred feet below me but they appeared to be a man and a woman. Eventually I met up with them and we introduced ourselves and shared our knowledge of the route. They had been up it years before but there had been no snow and ice. They did have ice axes and a rope and harnesses but no crampons. They elected to proceed and we parted ways. By now the slope had mellowed a bit and I was moving quickly over large talus. I lost sight of them as they entered the snowy section. I was back in the sun and really enjoying the day. I chose a different route to get back to the trail and enjoyed the exploration. I found a steep but passable section below a small mountain lake that led back to a bend in the trail. From there I could see the whole valley almost all the way to the parking lot five miles or so below. I made fast time down the trail. As I got within a couple miles of the parking lot I began to encounter other hikers and when I got to the parking lot it was nearly full. Another "failed" summit attempt but I was safe and I'd had a splendid day in the mountains.

After a few days I drove across Colorado to the southwestern corner of the state. My destination was Ouray, Colorado, a small former mining town near Telluride that now thrives on tourists, mostly in the summer. It is also home to the only man made ice climbing park in the country – at least to my knowledge. The ice climbing generally starts in November so I didn't get to check that out. My goal was Mt. Sneffels – a 14er that is only a few miles from town. I had no trouble securing a hotel room for the night and went for a walk about town. It reminded me a bit of Red Lodge, Montana but in reality there are many similar places in the Rocky Mountain west. I asked a few people where I should eat dinner and the consensus was the Outlaw Restaurant, a western saloon and steakhouse. I sat at the bar and enjoyed a terrific meal. The bartender was friendly and informative and the place was pretty busy for a weeknight in the off season. I was tempted to hang around and see what the bar scene would be like as evening turned to night but I needed to get up early for another alpine start so I walked back to my motel.

    4:00 AM came early. I downed a cup of coffee from the hotel room coffee maker and a bowl of instant grits, tossed my pack in the car and I was off to find the trailhead. Sometimes finding the trailhead is the biggest adventure of the day in the mountains, especially in the pre-dawn darkness. That's why I like to do some exploration the day before if time allows. The guidebook for Sneffels warns of a steep, rocky, narrow 4 wheel drive road with steep cliffs along the side. I was more than a little bit anxious as the road wound through the cold morning darkness – all alone on a somewhat treacherous road. The guidebook indicates that "rugged" cars should park at a dirt pull-out about a mile or so shy of the actual trailhead but that 4 wheel vehicles with plenty of clearance and a competent driver can proceed all the way to the trailhead. I was driving the Xterra but elected to park at the first parking area anyway. It was still early – around 5:00 – and the approach wasn't supposed to be that long. The sky was clear and beautiful as I trudged up the road. After about a half-hour walking on the twisting, turning road I still had not found the trailhead and the features I could see did not match up with the small map I had. Obviously I had made a mistake. I turned around and headed back toward the car.

    As I got within a few hundred yards of the car I noticed a turn-off in the road that I had not even seen on the way up the first time. The turn-off isn't mentioned in the guidebook. Sure enough there was even a sign that indicated this was the way to the drainage that I was shooting for. Unfortunately the sign had been partly knocked down and wasn't really visible unless I shined my headlamp directly on it – and even then only from one vantage point. Had I driven the car to this point I think I would have seen it in my headlights. By now the first light of dawn was

Clouds seething in the background, deer in the foreground on the approach to Mt. Sneffels

starting to erase the inky blackness of night. Dawn also brought with it overcast skies and an intermittent drizzle. It was about 6:00. I elected to use the car this time to go the rest of the way to the trailhead. The book was right. That last mile is among the most challenging that I have ever driven. It wasn't long though before I reached the trailhead. The trailhead is really just a pit toilet next to the road with a few parking places. The road actually continues on. I found out later that it is a 4 wheel drive track that is popular with tourists who sign on with excursion operators to ride in big 4 wheel drive vehicles. More adventurous types even rent vehicles and drive the route themselves. I was told that the route winds through the mountains and eventually reaches Telluride.

By now I could see that the entire sky was seething with clouds and mist. I decided to give it a go anyway since there would be no real danger (unless I encountered lightning – which seemed unlikely at this time of day at this time of year) until I got to the steeper section of the mountain. It was cold but not quite cold enough for snow. I put on a weather resistant layer and headed up the road. After about a mile and a half I reached a lake where the trail parts company with the road. By now I was approaching 12,000 feet and the drizzle was beginning to turn into

My high point on Mt. Sneffels – the summit looms behind me in the snowy clouds

snow showers. Another mile and there was nothing but snow – with limited visibility. I was still hoping the weather would pass and give me a shot at the summit. I had chosen a class 3 route to the summit up an exposed ridgeline with a class 2 descent down a talus/scree gully. These would both be far more dangerous if covered with fresh snow, especially alone. The snow showers turned into snow squalls and pretty soon I was trudging through several inches of fresh snow in my approach shoes.

    I reached a steep section of switchbacks which led to my ridgeline at Blue Lake Pass. This was the decision point. It was still snowing pretty hard at times and in the interludes I could see nothing but swirling clouds in every direction. I waited with my back to the wind-driven snow for about a half-hour to see if it might clear but my hopes dwindled as the minutes passed. It was a dramatic scene but it was clear that I would not be going any further. I took a few photos and reluctantly turned back toward the car. I had not seen anyone all day. The solitude was made even more striking by the splendor of the scene. During breaks in the snow squalls I could see the mountain tops that I was surrounded by piercing the cloudy sky. As I reached my car, another vehicle pulled into the parking area. It was a younger couple who planned to hike a ways up the road.

    As I drove carefully down the rugged track I encountered one of the 4 wheel drive tourist vehicles approaching from the other direction. I parked as far to one side as I could and let him pass. The driver/guide nodded courteously – one mountain lover to another - and the tourists in the back pointed and chattered with apparent curiosity. The snow at this elevation had turned back into rain. It was to continue throughout the San Juan Range all day and into the next.

Once I reached the highway I turned south and drove to Silverton where I had lunch and then on the Durango where I spent the night. The rainy drive was punctuated by snow at the higher elevations along the way. I had considered taking the narrow gage train ride between Durango and Silverton but decided against it based on the weather. The next day I drove all the way back to Boulder, this time by a more southerly route on mostly two lane roads.

Back in Boulder, I went to court with Austin for his Minor in Possession charge. I was surprised to see how many young people were there for drinking offenses. The courtroom was packed and apparently they hear such cases twice a week, every week. As it was his first offense, he was instructed to attend a class and the charge would subsequently be dismissed.

That weekend we attended most of the World Cup climbing competition at Movement Climbing and Fitness – the "showcase" climbing gym in Boulder. It was good to spend time with Austin doing something we both enjoyed and seeing well-known elite climbers from all over the world compete.

I considered driving the Xterra back to Virginia since I had revoked Austin's driving privileges. I also considered flying back and either taking the keys with me or leaving them with a friend in Boulder. In the end, I asked Austin if he drove me to the airport and kept the keys if I could trust him to not drive the car. He, of course, said yes and I elected to trust him.

Within a month I had become concerned that things in Boulder were not going as well as I had hoped. Although I had access to very little information, Austin's grades seemed to be a problem, and I wasn't convinced he was making progress on his school-imposed sanctions. I also suspected that he might be driving the car. I decided on a surprise visit and flew out there in mid-November, only a few days before fall break was to begin. I will not embarrass Austin here with what I found but suffice it to say that I was not happy. I left the next morning – this time with the car, which I drove all the way home. Austin flew home a few days later for fall break and the Thanksgiving holiday. There was much discussion in the ensuing week on what would happen next. In the end I elected to drive back to Colorado at the end of fall break and stay there with Austin in a motel through final exams in mid-December. While there I decided not to send Austin back for the spring semester. That decision didn't go over well with Austin. It was a turbulent couple of weeks.

During this time I was also training for my trip to Argentina, less than a month away. I ran most every day around Boulder or up in the foothills of the Flatirons. Some days I ventured off to Indian Peaks Wilderness or Rock Mountain National Park where I trudged through the snow or skied on backcountry skis. After exams we drove together back to Virginia. I was getting to know that 1,700 miles of interstate pretty well.

ROCKY STARTS AND A BIG NEXT STEP

Over the holiday Austin enrolled in some classes at one of the local community colleges for the spring semester and found a job waiting tables in a restaurant. I was not at a point where I could trust him to stay at my house alone so we planned for him to stay with his mother the whole time I was to be gone to Argentina.

Chapter 27

Aconcagua

Argentina
January, 2012

I left for Argentina on January 3rd and arrived in Mendoza the next day after stops in Miami and Santiago, Chile. Mendoza is the main town in Argentina's wine country and the gateway to the nearby section of the Andes Mountain Range. It is a thriving small city with a population of just over 100,000 and a metro area approaching a million. It has an interesting mix of first and second world infrastructure and even an element of third world, mostly on the outskirts. Our guides had made arrangements for us at one of the nicest hotels in Mendoza. It was terrific – lovely, spacious, comfortable rooms with views of the city, beautifully appointed public spaces, a pool, spa and excellent restaurant. We stayed here one night on the front end and one (or two, depending upon connections and plans) on the back end of our trip.

Once settled in to the hotel, our group met for the first time. This particular expedition was intended for medical doctors with an interest in altitude and mountain-related

LEFT Aconcagua, bathed in alpenglow, towers above base camp

maladies as well as wilderness medicine. A specialist in such things offered a series of lectures during the trip and climb for which the doctors receive continuing education credits called CME's. They pay extra for the classes. The specialist is none other than the founder and chief clinician at the Everest Base Camp clinic, Luanne Freer, MD. Proceeds from the CME fees go to support her clinic at Everest Base Camp. I'm not a doctor but Andes Mountain Guides (AMG) does not mind if non-doctors sign up for the trip. I actually got to sit in on all of the lectures. As you might expect a lot of the content was technical and required medical training but mostly it was very informative and Luanne made an effort to include me in the discussion. After the trip I made a small donation to her clinic – officially called Everest ER – to show my appreciation.

Our group was comprised of Luanne plus four clients and two guides. The other clients were Remi and Brittany, a recently married couple from New England and Ginny, a single woman from Australia. Remi is a 30 year old physician and Brittany – 25 years old as I recall - works in the non-profit arena. Ginny is a 36 year old physician with the Australian military. Remi and Brittany have the travel bug. They have both travelled extensively around the world and have more recently become interested in adventure sports. They actually met on the beach in Hawaii several years ago. Ginny hopes to climb the seven summits. At the time we met she had already knocked out two of them, Kosciusko in Australia and Kilimanjaro in Africa. She had plans to climb Denali (Alaska/North America) and Elbrus (Europe) in the summer of 2012. If she were successful on Aconcagua and the two planned for the summer that would leave only two – Everest (Asia) and Vinson (Antarctica). Our CME instructor, Luanne, is an experienced mountaineer, having summited Aconcagua the year before and having spent numerous seasons (March – June) at Everest Base Camp. She is also the chief doctor for Yellowstone National Park. Due to other commitments this year however Luanne would only be going as high as base camp with us. When we moved higher on the mountain, she would return to Mendoza to fly home.

Our guides were Mike "Coop" Cooperstein, owner of Andes Mountain Guides, and Leo Rasnik, a local guide who frequently works for AMG during the Aconcagua season (December – February). Both of our guides had summited Aconcagua several times among numerous other accomplishments in the mountains.

Our group convened in the lobby of the hotel. After introductions Coop gave us a quick rundown on our plans for the next few hours and days. Leo was with his family and would join us the next morning. There was much to do. First Coop came to each of our rooms to inspect our clothing and gear. No one wanted to find out when it was too late that they were not adequately prepared. Sub-zero temps are not uncommon high on the mountain even in the southern hemisphere summer and proper boots, ice axes and crampons are important. Even the basics like containers for hot and cold water and eating utensils need to be checked. After that we would convene for dinner at a nearby restaurant and the next day we would venture across town to obtain our climbing permits – a bit of a bureaucratic boondoggle – before packing up in a large van with a trailer for our gear. On the way out of town we would stop to pick up our provisions and then head up into the mountains. The second night we were to stay in a lodge in the small ski resort of Penitentes. The day after that we would begin hiking into the park.

    Gear inspections went well and we all met again in the lobby to go to dinner at a nearby restaurant. I speak no Spanish but several members of our group did so interpreting the menu and ordering was no problem. We got to know a little more about one another over several bottles of wine. I was the oldest member of our group. Luanne isn't much younger than me (I was surprised to find out since she looks considerably younger than she is) but the others are much younger – 20 years and more. I was in pretty good shape but it wasn't lost on me that the rest of the team could be in better shape. I didn't want to hold anyone back. By the end of dinner I was satisfied that there did not appear to be any troublesome personality issues and everyone seemed to get along well. As far as I know everyone turned in right after dinner. I know I did. I hadn't gotten much sleep since leaving home more than 40 hours earlier.

    The next morning we met for breakfast in the hotel. They had a terrific buffet – that included mimosas! This would be our last really good meal for several weeks and I think we were all aware of that. Leo arrived while we were eating and he proved to be delightful. I don't know that I have ever met a more energetic, upbeat person – but not to the point of being annoying. We set off to take on the Argentinian bureaucracy and before long we each had a permit to climb Aconcagua – to the tune of $700 US each. We hoofed it back to the hotel where the van was waiting.

We had all of our gear loaded in no time and we were off to pick up provisions across town. After that quick stop we headed out onto the highway and the roughly 6 hour drive to Penitentes. Along the way we stopped at a restaurant famous for its Argentinian steak. What it lacked in tenderness it made up for in volume. Each steak must have weighed a pound or more and was accompanied by about a pound of very tasty French fries. During the drive Luanne provided the first few CME lectures so the time went by fairly quickly. As we got close to Penitentes clouds rolled in and it started to drizzle but the forecast called for clearing overnight and a nice day the next day.

We had packed our gear into three loads. The first load were things that we would not need until higher on the mountain – big packs, warm clothing and mountaineering equipment – as well as the group gear – tents, food, fuel, etc. Those duffels would be delivered to us at base camp – 14,340'. A second smaller duffle included things we would need at the intermediate camp – 11,090' – sleeping bags, toiletries, etc. Finally our personal items for the approach stayed in small daypacks – snacks, a layer or two, sunscreen, hats, water bottles and so forth. As we unloaded from the van we were careful to put our loads in the correct piles for the expedition service to pick up and deliver to us on the mountain. Considering the number of people on the mountain in various stages of their expeditions it is remarkable that the logistics, at least for us, went off without a hitch.

In stark contrast to our accommodations the night before, the ski lodge we stayed in this night was a dump. It appeared to be the only game in town though as essentially everything else closes down at the end of ski season. It isn't really a town. In fact Ginny and I walked from one end to the other in about 10 minutes. We did find a place to get a snack and drink a beer before we rejoined the rest back at the lodge. The lodge serves dinner and a buffet breakfast in their dining room. I would say the food is somewhat hit or miss at best but the staff is cheerful and they seem to try to do the best they can with what they've got. The owner, a German guy in his early 40's, recently acquired the place through a lease agreement and seems determined to turn it around. I hope he's successful but it looks like an expensive proposition to me.

The next morning after breakfast, we hopped in another van with just our daypacks. Our other loads had been picked up by the expedition service during the night and would be moved up the mountain by mules. The van

The team sets out from the park entrance

took us to the park entrance a few miles away, with one short stop to pick up bag lunches and some snacks. Pretty soon we were marching off toward Confluencia, first stop for climbers and base camp for lower altitude trekkers. It is a pretty mellow 5 mile hike with only about 2,000 feet of elevation gain – to a bit over 11,000'. We set up the tents that had been delivered by mule team earlier in the day then settled into an expedition service dome tent for snacks and dinner. Confluencia camp actually has toilets that flush – something I had never seen in the backcountry before. This minor miracle is made possible by tapping into glacier melt a little higher on the mountain and piping it into camp via gravity-fed plastic pipe. The toilets empty into a rudimentary septic system. The whole thing is a bit of a jury rig but it is impressive.

The next day we went on a day hike to begin our acclimatization process. The expedition service provided us with bag lunches of sandwiches and hard candy. Our objective was Plaza Francia which has a spectacular vantage of the daunting south face of Aconcagua. The hike is about 7 miles each way with about 2,000 feet of elevation gain – to an altitude of 13,400. When the south face of Aconcagua came into view – the first time any of us (except Luanne and the guides) had ever actually seen it – I was struck by the magnitude of what I had taken on. The summit towered some 9,400' above us at the top of a very steep and snow covered wall. That was where my friend Juan (Coop's partner) had spent an unplanned (and unpleasant) night on a ledge and lost parts of several of his fingers as a result. I looked around at my climbing partners. We were all in awe. We sat in the lee of a large boulder, protected from both the sun and the wind for nearly an hour gawking at the massive mountain before us. Our route to the summit would be far less direct (and less technical and dangerous) than the steep and treacherous south face our eyes were glued to. We would traverse almost all the way around the mountain to the west and "attack" it from the north via a much less steep approach. Eventually we rose and began the trek back to Confluencia. I wondered on the way back if I really had it in me to go up that mountain. I suspected that I wasn't the only one.

As our team became better acquainted, we developed a lively banter. Luanne was the instigator of much of our dialogue. She has a terrific and slightly off-color sense of humor and a knack for knowing just how far she can go without offending anyone. I became quite fond of her in just a short time. Even though she doesn't look it, she is closer to my age than to the rest of the team. She is obviously smart and has tons of backcountry and high altitude mountain experience. Unfortunately for me, she is happily married. Her husband is a lucky guy!

How many mountaineers does it take to set up a tent?

Back at Confluencia we checked our SpO2, pulse and other health indicators. SpO2 is a measure of the amount of oxygen in the blood. At higher elevations, all else being equal, oxygen saturation in the blood tends to go down. "Normal" SpO2 readings are generally in the high 90's (expressed as a percentage of maximum possible saturation). At high altitudes it can drop all the way down into the 50's. Pulse on the other hand tends to increase at altitude as the heart races to compensate for the diminished oxygen content of the blood. We also tracked routine body functions – urination and defecation – as altered routines can be a sign of trouble. It is particularly important to stay hydrated and urination is an obvious indicator. We executed this routine every evening before dinner and Coop recorded all of the data.

Dinners in the expedition service camps always included soup – made from powdered soup mix, perhaps with a smattering of fresh vegetables or canned meat. The main course ranged from steak (rawhide?) to chicken to pasta and pizza. The food was good considering the resources available. They even had vegetarian options. Luanne is a quasi-vegetarian apparently. Breakfast was either scrambled eggs (from containers) or something they called porridge which was kind of like a cross between oatmeal and grits. The lunches they provided were always the same – dry ham and cheese sandwiches, hard candy and occasionally an apple. We drank bottled water at Confluencia but once we got a bit higher on the mountain we drank mostly water from the streams that flowed unimpeded from melting glaciers. We never treated it and no one got sick.

The next day we were up early to pack our tents and gear in time for the mule team to pick it up on their way up the mountain. During the climbing season numerous mule teams go up and down the mountain each day. The teams range from a handful of mules to very large groups – maybe 40 or 50. They start each day at the park entrance and go all the way to base camp and back – over 20 miles and 5,000 feet of elevation change in each direction. Some make a stop at Confluencia. Hikers must move out of their way as they move along the trail at surprising speeds.

The long hike to base camp

The hike to base camp – Plaza de Mulas – was long and grueling, about 15 miles with about 3,000 feet of elevation gain, most of it in the last 2 miles. The vast majority of the approach follows a fairly flat, wide glacial valley with (at this time of year) a trickle of a river running down it. There is very little vegetation and the scene is a bit "moonscape-ish." The earth has a red tint to it and it is very dusty. The valley is surrounded on both sides by steep cliffs of a variety of earth tones and the valley floor has a smattering of glacial eratics, boulders stranded by retreating glaciers many years ago. The sun is unrelenting and there is no place to find shade. Sunscreen, hats, sun glasses and buffs are de rigueur. Most of us wore our buffs in a way that covered our necks, ears and mouths and noses. It took a while to adjust to breathing through the fabric – in fact I never really did – but it does filter out some of the dust and helps retain moisture.

After trekking for what seemed like an eternity in this desert-like environment, the valley narrows and the trail starts to ascend. After passing through a constriction, the valley opens up again to reveal an enormous boulderfield. On the left side of the boulderfield next to the river are the remains of a building. It looks like it has been used for target practice by airplane bombers. It was actually partially demolished by an avalanche years ago – the 1980's I think. We stopped there for a short break. From here we could actually see Plaza de Mulas. Sadly it was still a few thousand feet above us – tantalizingly close but only accessible via a narrow, winding, steep trail up talus slopes and gullies. We had already been hiking for about 6 hours. It would be nearly another 2 before we dropped our packs for the day.

At last we reached base camp – Plaza de Mulas. I was pretty exhausted and I don't think I was the only one. Despite my exhaustion I was keenly aware that, at 14,340', I had attained the loftiest elevation I had ever reached (not counting airplanes of course). The expedition service was expecting us and had snacks spread out on a table in a big dome-shaped hut for us as soon as we shed our packs. Other climbers and trekkers were curious about the newcomers. Where were we from? What were our plans? Had we been here before? What else had we climbed? The routine is always the same when backcountry travelers cross paths away from civilization. People are sized up, stories exchanged and insight (beta) and suggestions are offered.

Before long we had set up our tents and were settling in to the routine of base camp. At least one member of our party took advantage of the hot showers offered by several of the expedition services. Water flows in to Plaza de Mulas through a network of gravity-fed flexible pipes that collect glacier and snowmelt several hundred feet higher on the mountain. Shower water is heated in large pots on propane-fired stoves then poured into large jerry

Snowy scene at base camp

cans which are hoisted onto a platform above each shower stall and attached to a shower head via flexible tubing. A hot shower goes for 10 bucks.

Toilets at base camp look like outhouses but under each one is a giant vat that collects waste. The vats are hauled out by helicopter every few days for disposal. It was an interesting operation to watch.

Base camp is surrounded on three sides by towering peaks, most of which are snow-covered, and cascading glaciers. The glaciers and ice falls have been receding in recent years but it is still a fairly impressive vista. While we were at base camp it snowed three times for perhaps a total of six inches or so. After the largest of the snowfalls the porters engaged in a massive snowball fight that seemed to go on for hours. The snow melted each time after a few hours once the sun came back out. Nighttime temps at base camp dropped to the mid 20's and daytime temps got as high as about 70.

The day after our arrival was a welcome rest day. We lounged around camp and enjoyed a few more of Luanne's CME lectures. We fell into the routine of base camp quickly. Breakfast was typically served around 9:00. Lunch was always a basic bag lunch – ham and cheese sandwiches. And dinner was the big treat of the day – generally served around 6:00 PM. After dinner we usually participated in a CME lecture then hung around and told tales in the hut until it was time to crash. The expedition services also provided wine. Most of us were pretty careful about drinking at altitude but a glass or two with dinner was nice and helped the group relax.

It wasn't long before a climber with another group took an interest in Ginny. I'll call him Friendly. He is an airline pilot from England and quite the physical specimen. He was the strongest and most experienced member of a three person team who had connected on the internet where they made plans to climb Aconcagua together (unguided) and met face-to-face for the first time in Argentina. Another man, also strong – and quite charming – was from Iceland. And the third member of the team was a young woman – early to mid 20's – from western Canada. Our itineraries for the ascent were not identical but there was a great deal of overlap and we often found ourselves in the same place on the mountain. The evolution of the romance between "Friendly" and Ginny provided some light drama and was the source of much speculation, not to mention gentle ribbing. Some members of our team jokingly pitted me against "Friendly" for the attention of the lovely Ginny. I can't emphasize "jokingly" enough since I am considerably older than Ginny and nowhere near the physical specimen that "Friendly" presented.

The day after our first rest day our plan was to summit one of the lesser summits nearby – Cerro Bonete - and return to base camp. Bonete tops out at 16,500 feet and is reached via a winding trail that ascends steeply to the west of Mulas. We were on our way shortly after sunrise. Along the way, only about a half mile from camp, is a vacant building that served as a hotel for trekkers until recently. As we walked by it a helicopter landed briefly and then took off again. Helicopters coming and going in the morning hours is a fairly common occurrence at base camp. They occasionally venture higher on the mountain (but no higher

Looking back at base camp from the flanks of Bonete – Aconcagua towers above on the right

than 18,000 feet or so) to extract climbers in need of rescue.

    The upper reaches of the trail switch back many times across a loose, steep scree slope. The going is fairly difficult, not unlike the trough on Longs Peak. The good news is that you can go straight down on the way down, taking big plunge steps in the scree – almost like skiing without skis. It took us four or five hours to reach the summit. Our ascent was really our first meaningful test of exerting at serious altitude. Brittany had a bit of trouble with the altitude but everyone did well and made it to the summit. I was particularly impressed with Luanne. Not only did she never seem to get winded, she was able to carry on a conversation while under way at every stage of the hike. I won't reveal her age but as I mentioned before she is closer to my age than to the ages of the rest of our team. Not only does she look younger than she is, she performs like a much younger person too.

From the top of Bonete we could see almost the entire route we planned to ascend on Aconcagua, including the locations of each of the higher camps. It was more than a little bit intimidating. At the summit of Bonete we were at the same altitude as Camp Canada which would be our camp 1 – our first camp out of base camp. There were two more camps – and over 6,000 feet of elevation gain above that to reach the summit of Aconcagua. The snow line on the mountain at the time we were there was at Camp Canada. Everything above that involved snow travel. I was nervous about it but definitely excited to get started. I was feeling good.

It only took us a couple of hours to descend back to camp. That night we were all a little concerned about Brittany who seemed to be suffering from a bit of mountain sickness. Late that day and into the evening we experienced our first snowfall. The entire mountain we had just ascended was covered in snow and it remained that way for a couple of days.

The next day was another rest day. Rest days are as much about acclimatization as they are about rest. Each day our bodies were producing more and larger red blood cells to try to compensate for the dwindling amounts of oxygen available to our lungs. Brittany was feeling better. Unfortunately this was the day that Luanne had to leave us. She had become the unofficial "ring leader" of our group. She always had a word of encouragement and often a witty remark. We all enjoyed her slightly off color humor. Luanne is one of those people who can bring out the best in everyone around her. She was definitely going to be missed. The seasonal population of Everest - Sherpas, climbers, guides and trekkers - are all fortunate that she started the clinic at base camp there and that she is a presence in that unique community each year.

Speaking of clinics, there are two on Aconcagua – one at Confluencia and one at Plaza de Mulas. Climbers, trekkers and guides must check in at each clinic to get permission to proceed further along. Docs at the clinics check respiration, pulse and SpO2 among other things at each station. Trekkers cannot go any higher than Mulas. As far is the park is concerned the only difference between a climber and a trekker is which permit you purchased. Trekking permits cost less than climbing permits.

On the second rest day there was a fair amount of discussion regarding the hiring of porters. By now we had a pretty good sense of the challenge associated with hiking up the mountain. We still really had not carried any heavy loads though. We clearly had a long way to go – on steep terrain at altitudes most of us had never experienced – and porter assistance could dramatically improve our odds of success by limiting the size of our loads. Each porter will carry up to 20 kilos (about 44 pounds of stuff). Their fee is $100 per segment so the cost of one porter all the way to high camp and back to base camp is $600. Ginny and I decided to split a porter and lighten our loads by 20 pounds or so each. It made a big difference. Remi seemed determined to forgo the expense of a porter even if it meant that he would carry far more weight than his diminutive partner. Brittany is petite – maybe 5'2" and about 110 pounds - maybe less. Remi is tall – around 6' – and strong. Our guides had hired one porter to carry some of the group gear – tents, fuel, food, etc.

Our second rest day was day 8 of our expedition. On day 9 we did a carry to camp 1 - Canada Camp – at 16,570 feet, a gain of just over 2,200 feet from Mulas. We hauled a tent, some food and fuel and all of our mountaineering gear - ice axes, crampons and such up to Camp Canada. Most of the route beyond Mulas is steep and much of the first segment is a loose, rocky trail. Leo set a slow pace. At this pace each step is deliberate and distinct. There's almost a momentary pause between each step. The group forms a rhythm. Watching teams ascend from base camp is almost hypnotizing as their synchronized movement inches them upward. Of course the porters move at an entirely different pace, leaving most of the climbers in their dust. They are remarkable. I'm certain that Leo could easily keep pace with them should the need arise – and Coop would not be far behind.

I was barely keeping up with the rest of the team as we approached camp 1 and Brittany was lagging a bit behind. Coop stayed back with whoever was bringing up the rear. Once we got there we cached the items we had hauled to camp. We tucked them under the overhanging edge of a boulder and covered them up with a pile of smaller rocks. It would all be safe there until we returned a few days later.

I felt pretty good – no signs of altitude sickness – but I was definitely struggling to perform. It was difficult to sustain even the deliberately slow pace our guides dictated. I was glad to return to base camp and hoped that another

Camp 1

day or two of acclimatization would make a noticeable difference.

Day 10 was another rest day and on day 11 we packed up all of our gear. There were loads for the porters which were carefully weighed and loads for our packs. Pretty soon we were headed back up the trail to camp 1. This time my pack weighed more which slowed me down, particularly on the last few hundred feet of elevation gain. I was pretty tired when we got there but we needed to set up camp before we could rest. As we were pitching tents I started to get a headache – one of the symptoms of AMS. Many things can cause a headache though so I wasn't terribly worried. The headache was mild but I decided to err on the side of caution. I holed up in my tent and drank water to make sure I stayed hydrated. I also decided to start a regimen of Diamox (acetazolamide) - 125 mg 2x per day. Diamox is used both to treat AMS and prophylactically to prevent it. It is a mild diuretic though so it is important to pay extra attention to staying hydrated.

Meals higher on the mountain mostly consist of soup (from powder/mix), cheese, bread and meat. The higher one goes the less of an appetite one typically has so eating can become a chore. I ate a pretty good meal and also took some ibuprofen. Soon I was feeling better. Despite taking a sleeping pill I slept fitfully that night, another challenge at altitude, but I was feeling almost 100% the next morning.

Day 12 started with coffee and cereal bars followed shortly by breaking camp. Each morning that we moved we needed to break camp early in order to have everything ready that the porters would be carrying to the next camp. Once they whisked through camp and collected our loads they were on their way up the mountain, quickly leaving us behind. On we trudged to Nido de Condores - our camp 2 – at 18,270', a gain of only about 1,700 feet. At this point the mountain was covered in snow and the trail was steep and slippery in sections. The snow was soft so crampons were unnecessary but the going was slow and arduous. I was really feeling the effects of altitude. Even at our slow pace my heart was pounding away – probably in the vicinity of 150 beats per minute – to get enough oxygen to my muscles.

Looking toward camp 2 from camp 1

With rest and water breaks it took us about three hours to reach Nido. Nido is a pretty big camp, sprawling over a fairly large area. It is the highest point on Aconcagua to which helicopters fly, so rescues that happen higher on the mountain have to be evacuated manually to Nido before helicopter support is available. Many parties take a rest day or two and/or wait for a weather window here before proceeding higher. That was our plan as well, both for the rest and because bad weather was forecast for the next day. After a bit of rest it didn't take long to get squared away in camp. That afternoon we visited with friends from other parties who were also laying over at Nido and some of us even played in the snow. The romance between Ginny and "Friendly" continued but the youngest and smallest member of his team was struggling with altitude sickness. They were to return to base camp at least three times after moving up high on the mountain in hopes that her condition would improve.

Day 13 was a lazy day – mostly lying around in the tent. It snowed off and on most of the day and the upper reaches of the mountain were enshrouded in clouds all day. There was a cold wind which made potty runs particularly unpleasant. Day 14 was crystal clear – bluebird skies and very cold temps, in the low teens. We broke camp early, interacted briefly with the porters and started the steep march to camp 3, our high camp. We were bundled with warmer clothes, goggles, mittens and hats. I found the big mountaineering mits to be awkward – difficult to do anything in, from adjusting goggles to grasping my trekking poles. The sky was clear but the wind continued to blow for most of the day. The route was even steeper in this section and involved switchbacking numerous times up the snow covered slope. The snow was deeper too so each step was even more of an effort. With the switchbacking sometimes the wind was on the nose and sometimes from the side or back. When it was on the nose the going was particularly miserable.

Camp Colera – our camp 3 – sits at 19,620 feet, a gain of only 1,350 feet from Nido. At about 19,000 feet I really started to struggle. I was lagging behind the rest of the team. On the steeper sections I found myself stopping to take a breath, sometimes two or even three, after each step. Coop elected to move ahead with the rest of the group and Leo stayed back with me. We arrived at high camp about an hour behind the rest. It had taken me over three hours to gain only 1,350 feet. While I recovered quickly – and felt fine while at rest – I was very concerned about summit day which was on tap for the next day. I knew that I was not performing well at altitude and really didn't want to spoil it for anyone else. I didn't want to slow the group down or jeopardize the summit bid for the rest of the team. We had two guides and if anyone were to turn back on summit day they had to be accompanied by a guide.

Camp 3 - high camp

At 22,841 feet the summit sits over 3,000 feet above high camp. The route is very steep. Packs are a bit lighter on summit day but the round trip is a serious undertaking at that altitude. I quietly pondered whether I would make a bid for the summit the rest of the afternoon and evening. I doused my headlamp around 10:00. I slept fitfully if at all. I still wasn't sure if I was going to go for the summit.

Day 15 - at 4:00 AM Coop called out that it was time to get up. I was already awake. The plan was to eat a light snack then get busy dressing for the summit attempt – to include crampons and ice axe. I decided to stay at high camp. I felt good about my decision. Mountains for me had never really been about the summits. That's not to say that I didn't like reaching the top. In fact there is an enormous sense of accomplishment that goes with summiting a challenging peak. It's just that I've learned to be nearly as happy when I know I've challenged myself and done the best I can at the time and that I've made good choices relative to risk and safety.

I said a few words of encouragement to my tent mate, Ginny and rolled over to try to get some sleep. Coop came over to the tent as the group assembled and asked me if I was sure I wanted to stay. I said I was and he responded that he thought I had made a good decision. I wished the rest of the team well as the sound of their crampons crunching in the snow faded into the darkness.

A few hours later – after the sun had risen – Brittany and Coop re-appeared at camp. Brittany had decided to turn back a ways up the mountain. Coop rested for a bit and then headed back up the mountain again, in hopes of catching up with Leo, Remi and Ginny. He never caught up with them and turned back again before reaching the summit. Leo, Remi and Ginny successfully summited. They did not return to camp until about 8:00 that night – after a grueling 15 hours of wrestling with the mountain. Along the way they assisted in the rescue of a climber who had succumbed to HACE. The stricken climber made it back down to high camp that evening and on to Nido the next

Remi and Ginny at the summit

day where he was evacuated by helicopter.

    I knew that, despite some lingering disappointment, I had made the right decision. I felt – and feel to this day – an enormous sense of accomplishment for what I did achieve. 19,620 feet is over 5,000 feet higher than I had ever gone before and I had never spent nearly as many consecutive nights in the backcountry before nor had I covered as much terrain in a single outing. Heck, I had never even crossed the equator before. I had much to be happy about. I thought often of Austin during those two days above 19,000 feet. I had been completely out of touch for over two weeks and hoped that he was coming to terms with his new reality. I wished he could have been there with me many times. At the same time I knew that he would find and tackle his own challenges in life, starting with addressing the short term questions about school, lifestyle, friends and direction.

Day 16 was another spectacular day on the mountain – cold but crystal clear. We planned to march all the way back to base camp – Plaza de Mulas – in one day. There had been no new snow in several days and the wind, sun and freezing temps had made the snow that was there crusty and dangerous. Crampons were required for the first section of the journey back to Nido. We moved slowly for safety's sake but it was downhill so the going was much easier than a few days before. By the time we got to Nido the sun had softened the snow a bit and we were able to shed our crampons. A ways below Nido most of the team elected to take the more direct route straight down the mountain – plunge stepping in the snow and later in the loose scree. I did a bit of that but after landing flat on my back a few times I decided to back off and switchback my way down. I just didn't have the stamina of the younger members of our team. It took longer but it was much less tiring – and entailed less risk of getting hurt. Coop stayed back with me.

From high camp to base camp took us about five and a half hours. Coop and I arrived about 45 minutes behind the others. Spirits were high but we were all a bit exhausted – especially me. And we knew we had to hike all the way to the park entrance the next day – a trek of over 20 miles.

Day 17 – We covered the distance to the park entrance remarkably fast – around six hours if I recall correctly, including rest and lunch stops. We then spent another night at the lodge in Penitentes where things were

239

about the same as before. They had experienced a mechanical problem of some sort in the kitchen that afternoon and weren't sure if the dining room was going to open that night. At 7:00 PM it was still "touch and go" but fortunately the wine was flowing. Shortly after that they announced that the kitchen would open and they began seating people. It was after 10:00 when we finally finished dinner. Happily there was plenty of wine.

Day 18 – The van drove us back to Mendoza. There was talk of good food, massages and relaxing by a swimming pool – and of course talk of what we were all going to do next. Remi and Brittany wanted to learn to rock climb and Remi was eager to pursue paragliding which he had tried on a recent trip to Europe. Ginny planned to climb Denali and Elbrus in the spring which would give her two more of the seven summits for a total of five. I decided to take a cruise. I was ready for my first "leisure" vacation in over 15 years.

Back at the luxurious hotel in Mendoza I made an appointment for a massage and drank a couple of cold beers by the pool while I waited for my massage. The massage was just what I needed to work the kinks out of my sore muscles. Afterward I had time for a nap before we all headed out to one of the nearby vineyards for a celebratory team dinner. We toasted our safe adventure on the mountain and the successful summit bids of Leo, Remi and Ginny and thanked our guides Coop and Leo. It was a memorable evening.

Day 19 – Andes Mountain Guides builds one extra day in their itineraries for bad weather and delays so we all had a day to kill the next day. I spent most of the day by

Time to celebrate – left to right: Remi, Ginny, Coop, Leo, Manson and Brittany

the pool. We met again for an informal dinner that night at a restaurant near the hotel. Leo had left the night before to rejoin his family at their home outside of Mendoza but the rest of us were still around.

Day 20 – We all went our separate ways. I flew back to Richmond by way of Santiago and Dallas, arriving the following day.

Chapter 28
Since Then

*I*n March, I went on a Caribbean cruise. It was far from what I was used to but the scenery was beautiful, the environment relaxing and the accommodations luxurious. I did a biking tour of San Juan, Puerto Rico and climbed the volcano in St. Kitts along the way. There was also an extensive fitness center on the ship so I was able to stay active but I'm not sure I would recommend going on a cruise solo. Everyone else on the ship was part of a couple or family so socializing was a bit awkward.

In an email exchange with Ginny recently, she informed me that further interaction with "Friendly" had revealed that he is an "elite pickup artist" – an experienced "ladies man" who likes to brag about his exploits on a website for like-minded men. Who knew that such a website even existed? Ginny summited Elbrus in July but her summit bid on Denali was not successful. Weather and other issues on the mountain conspired to foil her group. I believe she got as high as 16,200 feet.

As I put the finishing touches on this book, it is September, 2012 – 9 months since the trip to Argentina and Aconcagua. Austin is studying at Virginia Commonwealth University here in Richmond and living with me. I spent three weeks out west in August – about 10 days in and around Bozeman, Montana – a bit of it with Coop and a few days with Susanne who had flown in for another (successful this time) attempt on Granite Peak – and about 10 days in Canada – in and around Canmore, Banff and the Bugaboos with Bill and Adam. I've decided that major summits – altitudes over 15,000 feet or so and multi-week forays into the mountains – are not really my thing. I plan to continue to rock climb and bag peaks that can be attained in one to five days for many years to come. Austin will turn 20 in November. After one stumble in the spring, he has settled into a responsible routine of both full time school and a full time job waiting tables in a neighborhood pub. He's enthusiastic about his new school and his future, and I'm optimistic that he's turned the corner to a more mature, responsible lifestyle. I have plans to go back to Montana in February, 2013 – this time to ski at Big Sky resort. There's talk of a trip to Alaska next spring. Who knows, maybe there will be another book! Stay tuned.